P9-ECV-195

THE HERESY OF FORMLESSNESS

MARTIN MOSEBACH

THE HERESY OF FORMLESSNESS

The Roman Liturgy and Its Enemy

Translated by Graham Harrison

IGNATIUS PRESS   SAN FRANCISCO

Title of the German original:
Haeresie der Formlosigkeit: Die römische Liturgie und ihr Feind
© 2003 by Karolinger Verlag, Vienna
(Translated from the Third, enlarged edition)

Art Credit:
Christ of the Book of Revelation, surrounded by the symbols
of the Evangelists. Royal Portal
(panel on right purposely blurred)
Thirteenth century, A.D.
Chartres Cathedral, France
© Erich Lessing/Art Resource, New York

Cover design by Roxanne Mei Lum

© 2006 by Ignatius Press, San Francisco
All rights reserved
ISBN 978-1-58617-127-8
Library of Congress Control Number 2005938824
Printed in the United States of America ∞

For Robert Spaemann, in gratitude

CONTENTS

FOREWORD

Martin Mosebach insists that he is "not a theologian" but rather "someone whose task is to portray people and reconstruct human motivation". While this is technically true, it is overly modest.

Martin Mosebach is an accomplished novelist and writer. He is also someone who has read widely in the Catholic tradition. And as a novelist with a practiced imagination and a keen eye for the deeper meanings embodied in apparently ordinary human experiences as well as in extraordinary ones, he is particularly qualified to speak with authority on what meanings are in fact expressed by external acts, including the highest of external acts, which we call the Sacred Liturgy.

As a lay Catholic, even though a widely traveled one, Martin Mosebach has experienced two forms of the liturgy of the Roman Rite: the form that was universal prior to the missal promulgated by Paul VI in 1969 and the liturgy of the "*Novus Ordo*" Mass, as it is *almost* universally celebrated in the Latin Rite. I have emphasized the word "almost" for a reason that will become evident shortly.

Whereas from a strictly theological view, there is a continuity in the underlying doctrine and structure of the celebration of the Mass in its preconciliar and postconciliar forms, there have been so many changes, large and small, in the manner of celebration, that even a rubrically correct and reverently celebrated *Novus Ordo* Mass *appears* and is *experienced* by those with a deep understanding and appreciation for the Church's liturgical tradition as a "rupture" or "break" with tradition (both words have been used by then-Cardinal Joseph Ratzinger).

As an artist himself with an appreciation for form and beauty as revelatory of inner meaning, Mosebach decries the spiritual impoverishment evident on the experiential level in the manner of the celebration of the *Novus Ordo* Mass. On this basis he is convinced—and quite convincing—that the Church needs to return to preconciliar liturgy.

There is, however, a *tertium quid*. It has been variously described, but the label that has been most commonly used and is the most expressive is "the reform of the reform". There has been a lively debate, especially in English-speaking lands, between those who, like Mosebach, advocate a return to the preconciliar liturgy and those who, like myself, the Adoremus Society, and—I think I can assert this with confidence—Pope Benedict XVI, advocate a rereading and restructuring of the liturgical renewal intended by the Second Vatican Council, but in the light of the Church's two-thousand-year tradition.

These two positions are not as far apart as they might appear. The Second Vatican Council clearly called for some modest reforms in the liturgy, but it intended them to be organic and clearly in continuity with the past. Most of those who call for a return to the preconciliar liturgy will accept the kind of organic growth and change that has characterized the liturgy from its beginning. Those who advocate the reform of the reform want to see the present *Novus Ordo* Mass celebrated in a way that makes visible the deeper christological continuity with the Church's celebration of the Eucharistic Sacrifice of the Mass over the millennia.

Cardinal Ratzinger called attention to this deep christo-logical continuity in his *Spirit of the Liturgy*, when he evoked "the real interior act" of Jesus' "Yes" to the Father on the Cross that takes all time into his heart (pp. 56–57). This is the "event of institution" that assures organic continuity down the ages.

It is possible to make this profound reality visible by cel-ebrating the *Novus Ordo* Mass in ways that make the con-tinuity with tradition much more obvious. The *Novus Ordo* permits that Mass be celebrated with all its parts, or the canon and ordinary parts, in Latin. It permits Mass to be celebrated *ad orientem* (facing the Lord); the traditional first canon may be used; Gregorian Chant is still to be given "pride of place"; incense may be used and sacred polyph-ony sung; altar boys, bells, patens, communion rails where people may kneel if they choose, beautiful and noble vest-ments and sacred vessels; all this is permitted in the *Novus Ordo*. Permitted, but too rarely experienced.

We at Ignatius Press are proponents of a reform of the reform rather than mere restoration, even if the universal permission to celebrate the Mass in its "extraordinary form" may be the best means of ultimately achieving this desired reform. Why, then, would we publish a book by someone like Martin Mosebach, who argues so vigorously and elo-quently for a restoration? The answer is to some extent personal.

When I read Martin Mosebach's book in German, I was extremely impressed and profoundly moved by his under-standing and articulation of what has gone wrong with the postconciliar liturgical reform. After decades of the Church's establishment and even some official Church documents sing-ing the praises of the wonderful benefits of the *Novus Ordo* as celebrated, here is someone who puts into words and images the malaise that is still felt by many, and most particularly by those who cherish the richness and beauty of the Church's liturgical, musical, and artistic past.

We do not concur with every particular judgment Martin Mosebach makes or every conclusion he comes to. But we believe he has eloquently expressed a genuine and profound problem at the heart of the Church's life. We hope that this book will contribute to the new "liturgical movement" that Cardinal Ratzinger called for in his own liturgical *magna carta*, *The Spirit of the Liturgy*.

Fr. Joseph Fessio, S.J.
Editor-in-Chief, Ignatius Press

I

Eternal Stone Age

I am not a convert or a proselyte. I have had no sudden and spectacular illumination. My roots in religion were feeble for a long time. I cannot say with any certainty when they began to grow; perhaps it was when I reached twenty-five. At any rate, slowly but surely, they did begin to grow. I am inclined to think that these roots are deep by now and are continually growing, though, as before, in a way that is hardly ascertainable. What set this process in motion—a process that has not yet reached its end—was my acquaintance with the old Catholic liturgy.

My Catholic mother kept her distance from religion; my Protestant father maintained his right to his own private priesthood and defended it with iron discretion. Initially I learned very little about Catholic ritual because the preparation for the liturgy we received (supposedly suitable for children) practically obscured it with hymns saturated with optimism and pseudo-naïve prayers that could accommodate answers of opposite tendencies. As an altar boy I was the object of dread, since I had not grasped the structure of the rite and was always making myself a nuisance by doing unexpected things and forgetting important ones. One day, while the priest was praying, I snatched the huge Missal from under his nose intending to carry it to the other side of the altar (at what was altogether the wrong moment), tripped on my violet soutane, which was too long for me, and fell down the altar steps together with the book. That was the end of my career as an altar server. My "religious life" became rather pale after that, although the feeling of being a Catholic stayed with me. When I was eighteen I read the famous utterance of Charles Maurras: "I am an atheist; of course, a Catholic atheist." I liked that. I used to take pleasure in quoting it; it sounded rather daring. At the time I had no idea what atheism was, for I had an infinite trust in the world's goodness and beneficial order; as for the Catholic religion, I could not know what it was because no one had really told me. The Catholic religion is probably the most complicated religion in the world; to be a Catholic one needs either to be a recipient of a special grace or to have a great deal of knowledge; and I am a long way from either of these.

When I was eighteen the Catholic Church, too, was going through her own '68 craze. I was not very aware of this, for I was no longer going to Mass. But I heard people say that the priests had taken off their black suits and soutanes and went about dressed like petty-bourgeois students or petty-bourgeois postmen; there was no more Latin in the Mass; the priest no longer stood facing the altar but stood behind it, as if he were behind a counter; the congregation had become the priest's audience, and he looked at them and happily bawled the hymns at them; at Communion he put the Host into their hands, not on the tongue as formerly. The people I knew welcomed these innovations as something long overdue, but even my mother was quite definite that no one *had* to attend that kind of thing. I recall similar conversations with older Catholics who were clearly pleased with the reforms while at the same time being quite determined that "they would not be going."

What first drew my attention to the Catholic liturgy was the ancient Catholic music, Gregorian chant. I can anticipate the superciliousness of certain readers at this point: "Ah yes, this man's an artist, trying to satisfy his aesthetic needs through religion." I admit quite openly that I am one of those naïve folk who look at the surface, the external appearance of things, in order to judge their inner nature, their truth, or their spuriousness. The doctrine of supposedly "inner values" hidden under a dirty and decrepit shell is something I find highly suspicious. I already believed that the soul imparts a form, a face, a surface to the body, even before I learned that it was a truth defined by the Church's teaching authority. Consider me a Mediterranean primitive, but I do not believe a language that is untrue, full of deceit, and lacking in feeling can contain ideas of any value. What applies in art must apply to a far higher degree in the public prayer of the Church; if, in ordinary life, ugliness shows us the presence of untruth, in the realm of religion it may indicate something worse.

Gregorian chant is not art music. It exists to be sung in every village church and every suburban church, in spite of the fact that some of it is difficult and requires practice—and people did practice it, hearing it every Sunday all their lives. Only later did I realize, however, that the liturgy and its music must not be regarded as an occasionally edifying or impressive concert or as a help toward meditation; no, it is something that must be practiced one's whole life long. The obligation to go to church every Sunday should be seen in connection with the liturgy: the liturgy must permeate our lives at a level deeper than deliberation and thought; it must be something that, for us, is "taken for granted"; otherwise it cannot have its full effect on us.

The reform—or rather, the tide of revolution in the Church—had largely abolished Gregorian chant. The fact that it was far more than fifteen hundred years old, its origins lost in history, told against it. What the bishops forgot was that this music had sounded strange even to the ears of Charlemagne and Thomas Aquinas, Monteverdi and Haydn: it was at least as remote from their contemporary life as it is from ours—for we find it much easier to tune in to the music of other cultures than people of earlier times did. I once found myself in a beautiful little church in the Rheingau where Gregorian chant had been given a niche as a tourist attraction, as a piece of folklore. Crowds came to this place—Kiedrich—when the weather was fine, but in the winter, when there was fog and black ice, the large choir sang to empty pews; the Sunday-excursion and wine-tasting atmosphere vanished, and the chant came out in all its purity. Perhaps it would not matter if no one came; perhaps it would be enough if the singers sang on their own. But "enough" for what or whom? At that stage I did not know.

Gregorian chant is music that is strictly wedded to language. Furthermore—and this is what makes it different from modern musical settings of poetry—it is wedded to a prose that is not lyrical, a prose that is sometimes quite dry. The language of the Old and New Testaments, of Paul's letters and of the Psalms, is not crafted rhythmically or otherwise fashioned according to artistic models. At the same time the texts themselves are sacrosanct and should not be changed or edited for compositional reasons. Each word must retain its prose accent, though Latin poetry does permit a degree of license for the sake of meter in verse. It is astonishing to

become acquainted with the huge variety of melodies that
are possible, given such a strict set of conditions. Gregorian
chant does justice to every phrase; nothing is purely orna-
mental; syllables are neither skipped over nor stretched out
for the sake of the melody, as is often the case in the greatest compositions of modern times. This music is like a stream:
it gathers itself, now flows swiftly, bubbling and gurgling,
then spreads out serenely. To anyone who has listened to
Gregorian chant for a considerable time, the more recent
Western music is bound to sound like sterile hack-work,
constructed according to standard models, with its math-
ematically calculated form, its mirror techniques, and its
crablike progress. In chant, it is as if the phrase is touched
so that it sings, like the string of a harp; whereas the musical settings of later arias and songs seem to be arbitrarily
stuck on to the words. In Kiedrich there was only one piece
that left the words far behind and, like an ancient skat, seemed
to use the words simply as the vehicle for the most beautiful long coloraturas that just did not want to come to an
end. This was the Alleluia between the reading of the Epistle
and Gospel. Only later did I learn from an elderly church
musician that the purpose of this song of the syllable in free
flight, placed between the explicit texts of revelation, was
to represent the ineffability of God, transcending all words.
When it came to the sermon, the priest laid his chasuble to
one side, showing that his remarks were not part of the
rite. He was a "conservative" man who loyally obeyed his
"progressive" bishop—against his own convictions—and celebrated the remodeled, amputated new rite, but in Latin
and with that sobriety he had learned in the traditional rite.
After long searching I discovered this ancient rite that, in
childhood, had been a closed book to me. When I did so,
it was under far from ideal circumstances, in a hideous chapel,

and accompanied by chant that was woefully sung, but nonetheless it signified the end of my Sunday morning trips to the Rheingau.

In writing here of my relationship to religion I made it a rule to say as little as possible about religion. The profession of faith that I frequently murmur to myself in Latin, or rather, that I hum to myself—since I find it easier to remember it if I hum it to its melody from the *Missa de angelis*—by no means contains all the things I believe. The *Credo* was worked out by the Church Fathers at the Councils of Nicaea and Constantinople in the course of discussions that were at times extremely heated, to say the least; but, for me, what comes first is a whole series of important articles of faith, carrying perhaps even more weight: the *Credo* is, in fact, only the capstone of my faith convictions. Thus, for instance, I believe that I am a man. I believe that the world exists. I believe that the impressions received by my eyes and ears give me adequate information about reality. I believe that a thought has just as much reality as a mountain. Everyone knows that there is no half-compelling proof for any of these articles of faith. Many of them seem to fly in the face of scientific probability. I understand very well that people have doubts about them; sometimes I am assailed by such doubts myself. But at a deeper level of my consciousness I brush aside all the imposing objections against the reality of the world and the reality of my own humanity, even though I cannot refute them. I am afraid I have to admit it: I am a Stone Age man. I have not succeeded in reconciling my intellectual concepts with my fundamental convictions, which are deeply rooted in the physical. I ought to have accepted, long ago, that I live in a chaos, that there is nothing in me that can say "I" apart from some neural reflex, and that every sense impression of this non-existent "I" rests only on illusion and deception; nevertheless, when I hear the blackbird's evening song, which, as we all know, is not a song at all but a "sonic development favorable to evolution", and when I hear the distant clang of the church bell, sounded by a machine that strikes a piece of bronze on the clapper, I hear these things as a message—undecipherable maybe—that is meant for me. People say, and I should have grasped it long ago, that the objects surrounding me have not the slightest significance, that there is nothing in them, and that what I see in them is what I read into them (and who, after all, am I?). Yes, I hear all this, but I do not believe it. I am still on the very lowest rung of the history of mankind. I am an animist. When Doderer says that "a piano stands there, keeping its furniture-silence", I feel understood. I believe so strongly in the piano's objective existence, in its fundamental otherness and different-ness, that I am bound to interpret its way of standing in the room as a conscious keeping-silence. A Mongolian shaman once told me that if a stone is dug out of the ground it is upset for years. I regard that as quite probable. To me, if I listen to that utterly unteachable organ that is my inner voice, the world is filled, in every last fiber, with a life that is a different life from mine. This life can even take non-corporeal form, for example, in words. Some words are as disobedient as goblins, stuffed full of mischief and willfulness going far beyond what they signify; they are petty demons of the world of words: we all know them, but each of us is surprised by them in different words.

I record this basic confession right at the start so that it will be easier to understand how the old Catholic liturgy (which most bishops have forbidden and many actually campaign against) affected me when, after basking in Kiedrich's Gregorian chant for years, I finally attended the old rite again. The collapse of the liturgy in the official Church has had one good result: the old rite is once again a real mystery, in the sense that it is celebrated in secret, as it was originally intended to be. The first grade of priestly ordination is that of the "doorkeeper"—it has since been abolished—whose duty was to make sure that the doors were closed to the unbaptized during the celebration of the mysteries. In the Orthodox Church, before the Offertory begins, the deacon still cries out: "Attend to the doors!" I am not going to describe how I first happened to come across the old liturgy; anyone who has had a similar experience will know how much chance—or providence—is necessary in order to come across this rite. I think, too, that anyone who attends the old rite for the first time without any preparation will be somewhat baffled by it all. He probably does not know Latin, and in any case the most important words are whispered; the priest's vestments may be striking and beautiful, but the congregation sees nothing of what the priest does, since his own body obscures the view. There is a splendid old joke about the Jewish schoolboy who happens to find himself at a Mass and afterward tells his father about it. "A man came in with a little boy and gave the boy his hat. The boy took the hat and hid it. Then the man asked the congregation, 'Where is my hat?' and the congregation replied, 'We don't know.' Then they collected money for a new hat. In the end the little boy gave the man his hat back, but they didn't return the money." As I have already explained, when I was a schoolboy my grasp of the Mass was only slightly better than the Jewish boy's. Now, however, I came to see why it is important to stretch children and make them deal with things that are as yet beyond them. What was a puzzle to me then continued to hold an unconscious but firm place in my mind. The priest's quiet movements to and fro at the altar, his bowing, genuflecting, and stretching out his hands, constituted an ancient tableau that, without knowing it, I had carried along with me ever since. The way the priest stood at the altar seemed to communicate a kind of tension. Above the altar in the church of my childhood there was a huge gray plaster crucifix in the Beuron style, and I saw this gigantic tree as an axis reaching up from the altar to heaven. But even if the crucifix on the altar is smaller, I still have this feeling of the axis, linked with a sense of undefined danger. Whenever the sacristan busied himself about the altar, bringing something or taking it away, I always watched him uneasily. Persons like this, with their busy and matter-of-fact way of handling things that, for the layman, are numinous and unapproachable, have always belonged to the Catholic world, with its "distribution of graces". Even in the sanctuary there are janitors with just as much dire sovereignty as their profane colleagues.

Now, for the first time after so many years, I was watching a priest in the magnetic field of the altar. The things he said and sang slid past me: they were not so important. What was important was the impression that he was *doing something*. His standing and stretching out his arms and making the sign of the cross was an action, a doing. The priest up there was at his work. What he did with his hands was every bit as decisive as his words. And his actions were directed toward things: white linen cloths, a golden chalice, a little golden plate, wax candles, little jugs for water and wine, the moonlike white Host, and a great leather-bound book. The altar boys served him ceremoniously, turned the pages for him, poured water over his fingertips, and held out a little towel to him. After he had raised the Host in the air, he avoided touching anything else with his thumb and first finger and kept them together—even when picking up the chalice or opening the golden tabernacle.

The belief that human actions can actually achieve something can easily be regarded as a kind of megalomania. All one needs to do, to be cured of this megalomania, is to visit the desolate site of what was once an ancient city, a Hellenistic metropolis full of art, wealth, energy, and invention. But there are many people who would reject the idea of angels and yet say that whatever was thought and created, in such a city, is still alive—inexplicably, but highly effectively—and constitutes the basis for new things that could not come into existence without this foundation. It is only a step from this idea to the assumption that material actions have effects in purely spiritual regions. People of all cultures have believed this; that is why, to them, the highest action, the epitome of all action—because it was associated with the greatest efficacy—was that of sacrifice. Sacrifice is a material action performed to obtain a spiritual effect. This connection is absurd only if your philosophy is Idealist. For Stone Age materialists like me, all matter is so full of spirit and life that they simply pour from it. The last Europeans to hold on to this backward mentality were probably the great still-life painters.

We shall leave aside, for the moment, the question of precisely *what* the priest was sacrificing on the altar. The main thing for me, at that time, was that he *was* sacrificing. One of the prayers during the Offertory reads, "Accept this offering, as Thou wert graciously pleased to accept the gifts of Thy just servant Abel, and the sacrifice of our patriarch Abraham, and that which Thy high priest Melchizedek offered to Thee, a holy Sacrifice, an unspotted Victim." Abel, the shepherd, had made a burnt offering of the firstlings of his flock and their fat on the altar of sacrifice; Abraham had been prepared to sacrifice his son and, then, sacrificed a ram in his place; Melchizedek, who was not of the race of Abraham, sacrificed bread and wine. Primitive religion, Jewish faith, and the Gentile world were represented by the three names in the prayer of sacrifice; human sacrifice, animal sacrifice, and the unbloody sacrifice were cited, whereby the unbloody sacrifice recalled the bloody sacrifice through its symbolism. It was clear to me that the Catholic Mass in its traditional form—unchanged for more than 1500 years—should be seen, not as the rite of one particular religion, but as the fulfillment of all religions, having absorbed and enveloped all of them. Taking part in a sacrifice of this kind, I was uniting myself with all men who had ever lived, from the most distant times until the present, because I was doing what they had done. Participating in the traditional Sacrifice of the Mass, I felt that I was a human being doing something befitting a human being, that I was fulfilling the most important duty of human existence—perhaps for the first time—and that I was doing this for all the others who did not want to, or could not, fulfill this duty. Forbidding people to participate in this Mass suddenly seemed childish, not to be taken seriously. I found similar ideas in the essay (recently published in German) entitled *Titanism and Cult* by the priest Pavel Florensky, who was executed in Stalin's reign; of course, as the words of a priest they carry greater weight than the private ideas of a layman:

> Our liturgy is older than us and our parents, even older than the world. The liturgy was not invented, it was discovered, appropriated: it is something that always was, namely, the distillation of rational prayer, more or less. The Orthodox faith has absorbed the world's inheritance, and what we have in her is the pure grain of all the religions, threshed free of chaff, the very essence of human kind. . . . So it is beyond doubt that our liturgy comes, not from man, but from the angels.

If we are to experience the Christian liturgy in this way, it needs to have been purified and refined, a liturgy from which every trace of subjectivity has been eliminated. Even in the earliest Christian times Basil the Great, one of the Eastern Church Fathers, taught that the liturgy was revelation, like Holy Scripture itself, and should never be interfered with. And so it was, until the pontificate of Paul VI. Naturally this attitude did not prevent essential modifications, but such changes as occurred took place organically, unconsciously, unintentionally, and without a theological plan. They grew out of the practice of liturgy, just as a landscape is altered over centuries by wind and water. In the ancient world, if a ruler broke a tradition he was regarded as having committed an act of *tyrannis*. In this sense Paul VI, the modernizer with his eyes fixed on the future, acted as a tyrant in the Church. Maybe the anthropologists will say, one day, that he was right to wield power in the way he did, but that means nothing to me. I shut my eyes to this attack on the divine liturgy. Stone Age men have an undeveloped attitude toward time. They have no idea what is meant by "the future"; and as for the past, they think it must have been more or less like the present.

2

Liturgy—Lived Religion

In 1812, in Carlsbad, Goethe encountered the young empress Maria Ludovica; when the empress heard what a profound impression she had made on Goethe, she communicated to him the "noble and definite sentiment" that she "did not want to be identified or surmised" in any of his works "under any pretext whatsoever". "For," she said, "women are like religion: the less they are spoken of, the more they gain." It is a fine maxim, and one that deserves to be taken to heart. However, I am about to ignore it by speaking to you about religion in its practical aspect, lived religion, that is, liturgy. Perhaps the greatest damage done by Pope Paul VI's reform of the Mass (and by the ongoing process that has outstripped it), the greatest spiritual deficit, is this: we are now positively *obliged* to talk about the liturgy. Even those who want to preserve the liturgy or pray in the spirit of the liturgy, and even those who make great sacrifices to remain faithful to it—all have lost something priceless, namely, the innocence that accepts it as something God-given, something that comes down to man as gift from heaven. Those of us who are defenders of the great and sacred liturgy, the classical Roman liturgy, have all become—whether in a small way or a big way—liturgical experts. In order to counter the arguments of the reform, which was padded with technical, archaeological, and historical scholarship, we had to delve into questions of worship and liturgy—something that is utterly foreign to the religious man. We have let ourselves be led into a kind of scholastic and juridical way of considering the liturgy. What is absolutely indispensable for genuine liturgy? When are the celebrant's whims tolerable, and when do they become unacceptable? We have got used to accepting liturgy on the basis of the minimum requirements, whereas the criteria ought to be maximal. And finally, we have started to *evaluate* liturgy—a monstrous act! We sit in the pews and ask ourselves, was that Holy Mass, or wasn't it? I go to church to see God and come away like a theatre critic. And if, now and again, we have the privilege of celebrating a Holy Mass that allows us to forget, for a while, the huge historical and religious catastrophe that has profoundly damaged the bridge between man and God, we cannot forget all the efforts that had to be made so that this Mass could take place, how many letters had to be written, how many sacrifices made this Holy Sacrifice possible, so that (among other things) we could pray for a bishop who does not want our prayers at all and would prefer not to have his name mentioned in the Canon. What have we lost? The opportunity to lead a hidden religious life, days begun with a quiet Mass in a modest little neighborhood church; a life in which we learn, over decades, discreetly guided by priests, to mingle our own sacrifice with Christ's sacrifice; a Holy Mass in which we ponder our own sins and the graces given to us—and nothing else: rarely is this possible any more for a Catholic aware of liturgical tradition, once the liturgy's unquestioned status has been destroyed.

I am exaggerating, you may say. You may say that, though worship has been laid waste, the Church's teaching on the sacrificial mystery has remained intact. You may point to the fact that the reformer himself, Pope Paul VI, affirmed the sacred and sacrificial character of Holy Mass; you may say that his successor, Pope John Paul II, did the same and that the new *Catechism* contains the unabridged teaching on the liturgy, in harmony with the Church's tradition. That is true; what the supreme teaching authority says about Holy Mass is the ancient Catholic faith. The very fact that the *Catechism* could be published and that, despite the innumerable compromises in its formulations and the woolly lyricism that covers its various sore points, it does constitute a compendium of traditional Catholic doctrine of the faith, is itself a miracle in these times of ours. Since this *Catechism* was published we can feel a little less ashamed of being Catholics. But what effect does it have in our Church, on ordinary days and holy days? When Tsar Nicholas I was introducing strict censorship, he explicitly excluded from it any book that contained more than a thousand pages: no one would read books of that kind anyway. It is an indisputable fact, I know, that people dip into the *Catechism* from time to time in our seminaries—at least for amusement; but I am not interested in that. I am not a theologian or a canon lawyer. I am a writer, and I must look at the world from a different perspective. If I want to know what a man believes, it is no good to me to go through his "club regulations"—if you will pardon the expression. I must observe the man, his gestures, the way he looks; I must see him in moments when he is off guard. Let me give you an example of what I mean.

Following the papal indult of 1984, Holy Mass was celebrated according to the old rite in a small, unusually hideous chapel on the second floor of a former Kolping house[1]

[1] A hostel for young Catholic working men.

that had been turned into a hotel. It was decorated with dreadful ecclesiastical art: a concrete Madonna in a geometrical style and a crucifix made of red glass that looked like raspberry jelly; these were the sacred objects honored by the incensation. At any rate, no one could have been accused of going to this chapel out of aesthetic snobbery; this cheap slur, so often leveled at those who frequent the old rite, could not be directed at the Frankfurt faithful. The lay people who assembled there did not know very much about how things had to be got ready; they did not know the sacristy customs and only slowly acquired the necessary knowledge. Then a group of women who were in the habit of praying together began looking after the altar linen. I would like to tell you about these women. One day they asked the person in charge of the chapel what happened to the used purificators, that is, the cloths the priest uses to wipe away the remains of the consecrated wine from the chalice. He told them that they were put in the washing machine along with the other things. At the next Mass the women brought a little bag they had made specially, and afterward they asked for the used purificator and put it in the bag. What did they want it for? "Don't you see? It is impregnated with the Precious Blood: it isn't right to pour it down the drain." The women had no idea that in former times the Church did indeed require the priest himself to do the initial washing of the purificator and that afterward the wash water had to be poured into the sacrarium or into the earth; but they just could not allow this little cloth to be treated like ordinary laundry; instinctively they carried out the prescriptions of an ancient rule—albeit one that is no longer observed. One of these women said, "It's like washing the Baby Jesus' diapers." I was a bit taken aback to hear this. I found this folk piety a little too concrete. I

observed her washing the purificator at home after praying
the Rosary. She carried the wash water into the front garden and poured it in a corner where particularly beautiful
flowers grew. In the evening she and another woman prepared the altar. Adjusting the long, narrow linen cloth was
not easy. The two women were very intent on their task,
and their actions showed a kind of reserved concern, as if,
in a sober and efficient manner, they were taking care of
someone they loved. I watched these preparations with a
growing curiosity. What was going on? All the accounts of
the Resurrection mention the folded cloths—"angelicos tes-
tes, sudarium et vestes"—as the Easter Sequence says. There
was no doubt about it: these women in the hideous, second-
floor chapel were the women beside the grave of Jesus. They
lived in the constant, undoubted, concretely experienced
presence of Jesus. They behaved with complete naturalness
in this presence, in accord with their background and edu-
cation. Their life was adoration, translated into very precise
and practical action: liturgy. Observing these women, it was
clear to me that they believed in the real presence of Jesus
in the Sacrament of the Altar. That shows what faith is: the
things we do naturally and as a matter of course.

Go to any city church: What do people do naturally and
as a matter of course? Hardly anyone kneels for the act of
transubstantiation; often enough, not even the priest genu-
flects before the transubstantiated gifts. A woman brings the
Hosts for the congregation from a little golden cupboard to
one side; she does so in a busy and confident way, as if she
were bringing some medication from a medicine cabinet. She
places the Hosts in the communicants' hands; few of them
show the Host the reverence of a genuflection or a bow.

People of aesthetic sensibility, much scorned and suspect,
are the recipients of a terrible gift: they can infallibly discern

the inner truth of what they see, of some process, of an idea, on the basis of its external form. I had often spoken with pious apologists about the situation I have just described—it is observable all over the world. It was painful for the clergy to talk about these things, but they were not willing to admit that there had been a loss of spirituality. Kneeling was medieval, they said. The early Christians prayed standing. Standing signifies the resurrected Christ, they said; it is the most appropriate attitude for a Christian. The early Christians are also supposed to have received Communion in their hands. What is irreverent about the faithful making their hands into a "throne" for the Host? I grant that the people who tell me such things are absolutely serious about it all. But it becomes very clear that pastors of souls are incredibly remote from the world in these matters; academic arguments are completely useless in questions of liturgy. These scholars are always concerned only about the historical side of the substance of faith and of the forms of devotion. If, however, we think correctly and historically, we should realize that what is an expression of veneration in one period can be an expression of blasphemy in another. If people who have been kneeling for a thousand years suddenly get to their feet, they do not think, "We're doing this like the early Christians, who stood for the Consecration"; they are not aware of returning to some particularly authentic form of worship. They simply get up, brush the dust from their trouser-legs and say to themselves: "So it wasn't such a serious business after all." Everything that takes place in celebrations of this kind implies the same thing: "It wasn't all that serious after all." Under such circumstances, anthropologically speaking, it is quite impossible for faith in the presence of Christ in the Sacrament to have any deeper spiritual significance, even if the

Church continues to proclaim it and even if the participants of such celebrations go so far as to affirm it explicitly.

I went to different parish churches looking for communion patens and discovered that, in my town, since the communion patens were no longer thought to be necessary, they
had all been handed in for melting down. I repeat that I
am not a theologian; but to me—someone whose task is to
portray people and reconstruct human motivation—if someone allows all the communion patens to be melted down,
he cannot possibly believe in the real presence of Christ in
the Sacrament. We believe with our knees, or we do not
believe at all. "I can't do anything about it," a friend of
mine, a Protestant woman, once said, "but I find it embarrassing when I see a grown man on his knees." This woman
had a greater understanding of the crisis in the forms of
worship than the eloquent professionals with all their archaeological talk of "thrones" and Resurrection gestures and
prayer postures. A man on his knees because he believes
that his Maker is present in a little white wafer: this is still
a stumbling block in many places, and we must thank God
for it.

I have described my conviction that it is impossible to
retain reverence and worship without their traditional forms.
Of course there will always be people who are so filled
with grace that they can pray even when the means of prayer
have been ripped from their hands. Many people, too, concerned about these issues, will ask, "Isn't it still possible to
celebrate the new liturgy of Pope Paul VI worthily and reverently?" Naturally it is possible, but the very fact that *it is
possible* is the weightiest argument against the new liturgy.
It has been said that monarchy's death knell sounds once it
becomes necessary for a monarch to be competent: this is
because the monarch, in the old sense, is legitimated by his

birth, not his talent. This observation is even truer in the case of the liturgy: liturgy's death knell is sounded once it requires a holy and good priest to perform it. The faithful must never regard the liturgy as something the priest does by his own efforts. It is not something that happens by good fortune or as the result of a personal charism or merit. While the liturgy is going on, time is suspended: liturgical time is different from the time that elapses outside the church's walls. It is Golgotha time, the time of the *hapax*, the unique and sole Sacrifice; it is a time that contains all times and none. How can a man be made to see that he is leaving the present time behind if the space he enters is totally dominated by the presence of one particular individual? How wise the old liturgy was when it prescribed that the congregation should not see the priest's face—his distractedness or coldness or (even more importantly) his devotion and emotion.

I can see the ironic smiles on the faces of progressive clergymen when they read this. "Are you completely unaware of the historical development of the liturgy? Do you seriously think Holy Mass came down from heaven in the shape of the 1962 Missal? Can you talk about the sacrilege involved in altering the liturgy, when Church history shows that the liturgy has been created by an endless series of alterations?"

I started out by saying that, whether they wished to or not, all adherents of the old liturgy had to become versed in liturgical matters so that they could resist the attacks made on the liturgy in the name of scholarship. These attacks have indeed been resisted; they have been unmasked and shown to be untenable in terms of scholarship. The name of Klaus Gamber should be mentioned here: he stands for all those who have untangled and banished the figment of pseudo-archaeology and craftily spiced ideology. We know which elements of Jewish synagogue worship entered into Holy Mass; we can

identify the parts that come from Byzantine court ceremonial and those that are from monastic usage and Frankish royal
ceremony; we are aware of the elements that reveal Gothic
and Scholastic influence and those that owe their insertion into
the sacrificial ceremonial to the *devotio moderna*. The Mass as
we have it in its most recent form, prior to the Council, is
not a classicist pantheon, to put it in architectural terms; or,
if we look at it with the cold eye of the liturgist, it is by no
means a faultless, logical edifice according to the canons of
the Golden Mean, where every detail can be referred in a
highly artistic way to the proportions of the whole. It is more
appropriate to compare it with one of our ancient churches,
its Romanesque foundations rooted deep in the earth, with
a Gothic chancel, a Baroque painting above the altar, and
Nazarene-style windows. One does not need to have the
reformer's deprecating eyes to see what is strange and illogical in the structure of the Mass. As everyone knows, it was
not intended that the priest, after incensing the altar, should
quietly say a psalm verse—which is actually only the antiphon
belonging to the entire psalm that accompanied his entrance.
Similarly, it is clear to everyone that the "Dominus vobiscum" and "Oremus" before the Offertory once introduced
the oration that is now missing and that what does actually
follow is another "stranded" antiphon to a psalm that is no
longer sung at that point. Again, it may seem strange that the
faithful are first of all sent forth—and it should be pointed out
that "Ite, missa est" does not mean "Go, you are dismissed",
but "Go, it is the mission: your apostolate has begun"—only
to be kept there while they wait for the blessing, and yet again
while they are given a second blessing in the form of the reading of the beginning of Saint John's Gospel. No doubt there
are more puzzles to be explained by those who are expert in
these matters.

However, while it must be said that, in its texts and its sequence of actions, Holy Mass has had substantially the same form for a very long time, it is also true to say that it had a different "look" about it in each century, as is clear from the church architecture of the various periods. Holy Mass in old Saint Peter's in Rome at the time of the emperor Constantine, in a basilica heavily draped with curtains, was surely redolent of something between a mystical mystery-cult and a patrician state ceremony. A Gothic cathedral in which forty Masses were being said at all its altars at the same time for the benefit of the poor souls in purgatory would have had a different atmosphere from the theatrical Baroque churches where the Sacrifice was offered to the accompaniment of highly dramatic orchestral music. And the rationalistic purism of the French Benedictine monasteries that celebrate the old rite today would be unimaginable in any century but our own. What point am I making? Of course the rite is constantly changing on its journey through the centuries! It does this without anyone noticing and without the process having to involve any arbitrary interference. Historical beings that we are, we are subject to the spirit of the age in which we live; we have to see with its eyes, hear with its ears, and think according to its mentality. Changes to an ancient action that are brought about through the shaping hand of history have no author as such; they remain anonymous, and—what is most important— they are invisible to contemporaries; they emerge into consciousness only after generations. Changes and gradual transformations of this kind are never "reforms", because there is no explicit intention behind them to make something better. A feature of the Church's most precious store of wisdom was that she had the ability to look down from a great height on this historical process, as on a broad river, recognizing its irresistible power, cautiously erecting dams here and there or redirecting secondary streams into the main channel. Since Holy Mass had no author, since a precise date could be allotted to practically none of its parts—as to when it originated and when it was finally and universally incorporated into the Mass—everyone was free to believe and feel that it was something eternal, not made by human hands.

This belief and feeling, however, is the crucial precondition if we are to celebrate Holy Mass correctly. No religious person can see *cult* in an event that is fabricated out of commentaries on Church history and the pastoral theology of the Reform. The whole thrust of *cult* is that, for the participants, it posits facts linking heaven and earth; and it does so authoritatively. If it cannot claim to be objective, uncreated, something axiomatic, it cannot—anthropologically speaking—be the object of felt experience. What I do *not* want to do, when participating in Holy Mass, is be "active", since I have good reason to distrust the instincts of my mind and my senses. What "active" role, for instance, did the apostles play at the Last Supper? They let the astounding events enfold them, and when Peter started to resist, he was specifically instructed to be "passive": "If I do not wash you, you have no part in me!" What I want to find in Holy Mass is the happiness of the man in the New Testament who sits on the periphery and watches Christ passing by. This is what Holy Mass is about, and that is why the Sacrifice of the Mass is seen in the context of the Jews' Exodus meal: "For it is the Pasch, the Lord's passing."

The fact that the old rite is there, present to us as something that has grown, is the sign, the pictorial expression, of its divine institution. We can say that, like Jesus, it is "begotten, not created". The cautious way all the popes prior to Pope Paul VI treated the Mass tells us that the Church desired Holy Mass to have this iconic quality and wanted to promote this specific impression. So, when we celebrate Mass, we must endeavor to forget everything we have learned about it from Church history. Its core is the revelation of Christ, and therefore the religious man will want to treat the Mass in its entirety as revelation.

If we aim to bring out the religious significance of ceremonies and rituals to enable them to fulfill their religious function, it is pointless to ask questions about the historical meaning of the individual prescriptions. Often enough, historically speaking, liturgical actions go back to particular practical necessities, to the particular architectural features of some Roman church, to customs of an agrarian society, or to particular local and quite secular usages. This is all very interesting, and indeed it is wonderful how closely liturgy's treasure-house links us to the past, to the vast army of the dead who were Christians before us and without whom we would not have become Christians: but from a religious point of view it has no value.

Just as noble metals are used to produce the sacred vessels, making something profane into something sacred, so too the contingencies and particular events of history have turned, in the liturgy, into something holy; and holy things must always be regarded and assessed in a different way from profane things. The Hasidic Jews, the exponents of Europe's last mystical movement, said that every word in their holy books was an angel. That is how I want to regard the rubrics of the Missal: for me, every prescription of the Missal is an angel. Once I have recognized that an angel is responsible for every liturgical action, I shall never be in danger of regarding liturgy as something lifeless or formalistic or as a historical relic, the meaningless detritus of time's onward march.

It also preserves us from the unspiritual, legalistic, and scholastic way of looking at things that judges the mysteries of the liturgy according to the categories of "validity" and "minimal requirements". It is not right—and from the perspective of the religious person it is absurd—to look at the Holy Mass as if it were some legally binding trade contract with its stipulations and necessary conditions. It is "necessary" for a priest to say the words of Consecration; even the new liturgy is not "necessary" in that sense. But to think in such terms is to overlook the whole nature of the sacrament! The Church's sacraments are continuations of the Incarnation, continuing acts of God's descent into the abundant world of forms of his creatures. God became man, not only in a man's heart and soul, but also in a man's fingernails and the hairs of his beard. The liturgy must be as complex and astonishing as the mystery of the God-man it presents in symbolic forms. And just as the woman who was a sinner washed the feet of this God-man, and the Apostle Thomas touched his wounds, the religious person, contemplating the body of the liturgy, does not ask whether he has understood everything correctly (nor does he wonder whether he is faced with things that are superfluous, subject to change, or dispensable): his whole desire is to venerate and love this body, even in its tiny and marginal parts.

We often smile at the way medieval people were fond of explaining mundane things in a spiritual way. For instance, if the nave of a church was not quite square with the chancel, people said that the whole church represented the crucified Lord, and the slightly crooked chancel was his head, fallen to one side. I think this is how we *should* look at things. It is the most effective way of filling a rite with prayer and thus uniting form and content. It used to be the priest's duty, as he put on each vestment, to recite a specific prayer that explained it. Long before many of the priestly vestments were done away with, this prayer had fallen into disuse. This, to me, is an example of what happens; once the chasuble is no longer understood as the "gentle yoke of Christ", it is just a more or less tasteful piece of textile: Why not leave it off?

I would like to use two examples to illustrate this meditative way of filling the liturgy with religious meaning. It concerns two liturgical actions that play only a small part, if at all, even in traditional circles. The first is the consecration candle that is still prescribed in the 1962 Missal. I have never seen it used. The Missal orders that, prior to the Consecration, an additional candle is to be put on the altar beside the tabernacle and that it should not be extinguished until after Communion, when the tabernacle has been shut. This candle upsets the symmetry: Why? It is quite easy, surely, to see it as Christ, coming to join the disciples on the Emmaus road or stepping into the circle of the apostles and then withdrawing from their sight. Once you have seen the consecration candle in that light, you are bound to regret its disappearance from the liturgy. Then there is the *bugia*, the candelabra that is held beside the bishop for the readings (and that cannot possibly make the page any brighter at a morning High Mass!): Is there anything to prevent us from seeing it as a pointer to the fact that Holy Scripture can only be read in the light of faith?

The great iconoclastic crisis in the liturgy does, however, present us with opportunities. Where everything lies in ruins there is nothing left to preserve; the only thing to do is to begin to build again. Furthermore, we must reflect on the condition of the buildings prior to their destruction before we set to work to rebuild them. Let me be quite frank: I am not nostalgic about the form of Holy Mass I experienced as a child in Frankfurt in the fifties. In explaining what I mean by this, I shall keep returning to the way the Mass is often celebrated, in today's Germany, in those circles that are faithful to tradition.

As a child—albeit a particularly unteachable and reluctant one—I never understood Holy Mass, no doubt because the whole liturgy took place in the distance, like a silent play, while, lower down the church, a narrator incessantly distracted my attention from the sacred actions by uttering prayers, meditations, and explanations that were frequently very far from being mere translations of what was being spoken at the altar in Latin. I particularly remember hearing lyrical (and quite ambiguous) prefaces, one of which referred to the little flowers, fishes, and birds that were praising God; I recall the never-changing custom of the congregation reciting the "short" Creed while the priest said the "long" Creed in Latin; I remember hushed commentaries during the Consecration, reminding me of the sotto voce radio reports of the papal blessing *Urbi et orbi*; in brief, I recall the honest and careful dedication of the people who were entrusted with these tasks, which were designed to arouse in me the appropriate sentiments. It was the picture of a Church that quite evidently no longer believed in the effect of her rites. Of course the priests have to teach, guide, and initiate the lay people, show them how to pray properly, and urge them to keep to it. At the time, however, I know I felt that the center of gravity was being shifted, especially during the sacred ceremonies. At the center stood, not the objective service of God, the sacrifice that was both owed to God and provided by God, but an increasingly anxious attention to the congregation. The triumphalism of which the preconciliar Church is so often accused had long ago acquired an over-insistent tone. I also clearly remember my growing sense of a bad conscience when I had to utter prayer-formulae that spoke of an ardent love for Jesus and unconditional self-surrender: on my lips, in the absence of these sentiments, they were lies.

This ministry that was concentrated, not on the service of God, but on the molding and direction of believing souls found its liturgical—or, more correctly, its antiliturgical—high point in the vernacular hymns that completely dominated the celebration of Holy Mass. I cannot speak about liturgy without referring to the question of hymns; I am aware that there is no common mind on this issue in traditional Catholic circles, but I ask those who disagree with me to have a little patience with my argument, which is that of a somewhat untypical layman. I am firmly convinced, in fact, that vernacular hymns have played perhaps a significant part in the collapse of the liturgy. Just consider what resulted in the flowering of hymns: Luther's Reformation was a singing movement, and the hymn expressed the beliefs of the Reformers. Vernacular hymns replaced the liturgy, as they were designed to do; they were filled with the combative spirit of those dismal times and were meant to fortify the partisans. People singing a catchy melody together at the top of their voices created a sense of community, as all soldiers, clubs, and politicians know. The Catholic Counter-Reformation felt the demagogic power of these hymns. People so enjoyed singing; it was so easy to influence their emotions using pleasing tunes with verse repetition. In the liturgy of the Mass, however, there was no place for hymns. The liturgy has no gaps; it is one single great canticle; where it prescribes silence or the whisper, that is, where the mystery is covered with an acoustic veil, as it were, any hymn would be out of the question. The hymn has a beginning and an end; it is embedded in speech. But the *leiturgos* of Holy Mass does not actually speak at all;

his speaking is a singing, because he has put on the "new man", because, in the sacred space of the liturgy, he is a companion of angels. In the liturgy, singing is an elevation and transfiguration of speech, and, as such, it is a sign of the transfiguration of the body that awaits those who are risen. The hymn's numerical aesthetics—hymn 1, hymn 2, hymn 3—is totally alien and irreconcilable in the world of the liturgy. In services that are governed by vernacular hymns, the believer is constantly being transported into new aesthetic worlds. He changes from one style to another and has to deal with highly subjective poetry of the most varied levels. He is moved and stirred—but not by the thing itself, liturgy: he is moved and stirred by the expressed sentiments of the commentary upon it. By contrast, the bond that Gregorian chant weaves between liturgical action and song is so close that it is impossible to separate form and content. The processional chants that accompany liturgical processions (the Introit, Gradual, Offertory, and Communion), the responsories of the Ordinary of the Mass that interweave the prayers of the priest and the laity, and the reciting tone of the readings and orations—all these create a ladder of liturgical expression on which the movements, actions, and the content of the prayers are brought into a perfect harmony. This language is unique to the Catholic liturgy and expresses its inner nature, for this liturgy is not primarily worship, meditation, contemplation, instruction, but positive action. Its formulae effect a deed. The liturgy's complete, closed form has the purpose of making present the personal and bodily action of Jesus Christ. The prayers it contains are a preparation for sacrifice, not explanations for the benefit of the congregation; nor are they a kind of "warming-up" of the latter. In Protestantism, vernacular hymns came in as a result of the abolition of the Sacrifice of the Mass; they were ideally suited to be a continuation of the sermon. Through singing, the assembled community found its way back from the doubting loneliness of the workday to the collective security of Sunday—a security, be it noted, that arose from the mutual exhortation to remain firm in faith, not from witnessing the objective, divine act of sacrifice.

There is no point regretting the Jesuits' decision, during the Counter-Reformation, to take the hymns that had played such a signal part in the success of Protestantism and use them in Catholicism. The pressure from Protestantism was immense. The future seemed to belong to Protestantism. People defended the liturgy, but it seems they did not really believe it had the power to reach the hearts of the faithful. The liturgy was not interfered with, but it was allowed to fall silent. It was enveloped in an architecture in which the imagination had run riot and accompanied by orchestral music of the most contemporary kind, virtuoso concert "Masses" in which the connoisseur could listen in rapt admiration to a coloratura soprano singing the *Agnus Dei*; it suffocated under the curtain of either elegant or naïve rhetoric, found in many devotions and forms of prayer that had been developed for the laity. Then came the hymns. Because they were not genuinely Catholic, because they were alien to the spirit of the liturgy and had arisen, not from a spiritual need, but from tactical considerations, they did not possess the often impressive artistic power of their Protestant models. Still, they were there: the sound of hundreds of people singing smothered the liturgy and obscured what was going on at the altar. Thus came about the ill-omened and oft-criticized "two-track" liturgy. It was clear that something needed to be done; but, as we know, it was the hymns that were victorious, not the liturgy. To put it crudely: the liturgy disappeared, and what did the congregation see in its place? A "presider" in billowing garments, his mouth opened in joyful song.

I am speaking here entirely from my own experience. Here is another example that showed me with particular clarity the difference between vernacular hymns and Gregorian chant. There is a particularly beautiful hymn that, by way of exception, does fit fairly well into the liturgy. This is the *Te Deum*, in its German form, "Grosser Gott, wir loben Dich!" [the English hymn "Holy God, We Praise Thy Name"]. After the priest has sung "Te Deum laudamus" to Gregorian chant, the vernacular hymn takes over, simply replacing the original Latin hymn, that is, neither obliterating nor obscuring anything. As a child, my favorite hymn was this "Grosser Gott, wir loben Dich!" I was profoundly moved by it. I sang it at the top of my voice and was aware that everyone around me was also singing it at the top of their voices. I was in a welter of maximum emotion; the bells rang, and it seemed as if the church roof would explode with this holy din, just as, long ago, the walls of Jericho had fallen down; at that moment everyone believed; everyone was resolute; we were all ready to give our lives for religion. Then the servers' bells stopped ringing; the next verses were not quite so well known; the singing was still strong but had lost its overpowering quality, and as people pressed out of the church they had returned to their usual state of mind. Enthusiasm was replaced with contentment, mixed, in the case of particularly hearty singers, with a slight sense of embarrassment.

How amazed I was the first time I heard a Latin *Te Deum*. It was a lengthy piece, hovering to and fro, with its feather-light questioning and answering, a mixture of psalm, litany, and profession of faith, that combined—in a decidedly playful way—ancient elements and the new elements of redemption. Hearing this *Te Deum*, the legend that Saint Augustine and Saint Ambrose had improvised it at the altar, each replying to the other, was self-evidently true. This hymn could only have come into being by the highest degree of inspiration, in what Hölderlin calls "Heilige Nüchternheit" [holy sobriety], in the presence of the Holy Spirit that calls for a complex kind of game. It was impossible to bellow this hymn at the top of one's voice. It does not address the collective; it does not liberate emotions. The Latin *Te Deum* takes both listener and singer gently by the hand and leads them to a high mountain, where an unlimited vista opens out before them. The heart of the Latin *Te Deum*, even if all the bells are rung during it, is silence.

I would like to mention another passage in this hymn that was bound to suffer when translated into German verse and yet is characteristic of the spirit of the whole piece. In the middle of the great hymn of praise we hear these words: "Dignare, Domine, die isto sine peccato nos custodire" [O Lord, keep us this day without sin]. It would be impossible to sing this cautious, measured plea, with its sceptical view of human nature, to the confident and assertive melody of "Holy God, We Praise Thy Name." It is a model of moderation, and yet at its heart lies a spiritual claim that far transcends the effect of the Jericho trumpets: it speaks of a day on which, as men praised God in the words of the *Te Deum*, they were without sin; was this not a day in paradise?

While making the strongest possible case for the use of Gregorian chant in Holy Mass, I am aware that I am arguing in favor of an old, an ancient tradition that, even before the Second Vatican Council, was in decline in many places. As a child I had no experience of it whatever; and many of those who did experience the preconciliar Church in her full glory do not regard Gregorian chant as the most pressing need today. The vernacular hymns have also created an intellectual and spiritual home for many people. It would be silly to lament the collapse and destruction of tradition while excluding from this lament the traditions one does not like. The holiness of tradition consists, not primarily in its utility and usefulness, but in its durability. Forms of prayer that, for a hundred, two hundred, and three hundred years, have become real houses of prayer that believers can enter with ease must be given the protection due to every object that is withdrawn from profane use and dedicated to God. Taking things that were once treated with reverence and are so no longer, profaning them, scrapping them, throwing them away, melting them down, and auctioning them off—this is pitiless and vulgar. After all the waves of destruction that have scattered our sanctuaries down through the history of our country, after the Reformation and Secularization with its hundred-thousandfold profanation, this is the most recent, equal to its predecessors in destructive power. Someone ought to draw up a list of all the altars smashed to pieces in Germany since the Council. Our restored churches, expensively fitted out according to the latest architectural fashions, often resemble carefully dissected skeletons, ready for a future life as museum pieces. No one who really believes in the power of a blessing, the power of prayer, would be so reckless as to scorn and wreck something that has been sanctified by prayer and "electrically charged", as it were, with graces. I would even go as far as to say that a false relic to which many generations have had recourse in distress, and which has helped them to turn their thoughts to God, has the same value as a genuine one.

What does this imply for the vernacular hymns? It means that, while I am clearly aware that the whole development of vernacular hymns is a baneful tradition, conflicting with the spirit of the liturgy, I would nonetheless always argue that it should not be interfered with, as long as there is any danger of harming a spiritual and intellectual reality that is anchored deep in the souls of believers. This is precisely the unsavory lesson of the last twenty-five years: those who destroyed the old, familiar forms of prayer, hallowed by long use, ended up by cutting off their fellow believers' path to God.

Inherited customs deserve respect for as long as they last. But what if the continuity has been interrupted? At the very outset I explained what it means when a tradition is interrupted, questioned, when it ceases to be something self-evident. And we must admit, with no beating about the bush, that the Roman liturgy's fifteen-hundred-year tradition has been breached, and breached irretrievably. Dismayed and speechless, we had to watch as the supreme Catholic authority bent its whole might—a might that has grown over centuries—to the task of eradicating the very shape of the Church, the liturgy, and replacing it with something else. Even today a vast, intelligent, and efficient organization of officials is ceaselessly working to transmit decisions made at the Council to the remotest village in the Andes and the most secret catacomb chapel in China. Recently, in a newspaper, a German bishop was describing the distress of Bulgarian Catholics, who are indeed faced with a thousand trials—but the gravest concern, apparently, was that the old Missals are still doing the rounds there! A highly placed Jesuit told me of a journey he made to Sweden with another member of his order; "of course" they went to the Protestant service and even to the Lord's Supper, and only when they asked to receive Communion in the hand was it obvious to everyone that they were Catholics! That is how the Catholic's visible shape has already changed. If anyone is determined to hold on to the classical Roman Rite; if, in spite of the depressing facts, he wants to maintain reverence and guard sacred space, he should realize that he must do this without having the least hope: all hope has been undermined, politically, historically, and sociologically. Those who remain faithful to the fifteen-hundred-year old rite of the Sacrifice of the Mass are living in a vacuum. This rite has been abandoned by the very hierarchy who were created to guard it. Priests who stay faithful to the liturgy are accused of disobedience and threatened with suspension; priests who want to remain obedient, but are not willing to relinquish the old rite, are gleefully ground down by what Carl Schmitt calls the "celibate bureaucracy". It is profoundly unreasonable to risk the peace of one's soul by taking up arms on behalf of the liturgy; but anyone who still wants to do it might as well do it properly—not for a vernacular hymn of the 1820s, but for the archaic and yet ever-young garment that encloses the sacred mysteries like a skin. To preserve the liturgy, it seems to me, is to restore it.

There are other ways in which the celebration of Holy Mass customary in traditional circles deviates from the real spirit of the liturgy, if I have grasped it correctly. The main complaint, as I have already observed in connection with the vernacular hymns, concerns the "two-track" approach: certain cultic actions or chants are performed simultaneously, although they do not belong together. For instance, even in places where the schola actually sings the prescribed Introit (and not a hymn), it is sung, not as the celebrant is processing in or while he is reading the Introit in the Missal, but during the psalm "Judica" and the *Confiteor*. The text of the psalm

"Judica" is so important, however, and so relevant to the spiritual state of those who have withdrawn from the world to step into the sacred space—"Quare es tristis, anima mea et quare conturbas me?"—Why art thou sad, O my soul, and why dost thou disquiet me?—that we should be able to follow it. The congregation should also have the opportunity to pray for the priest's soul in the *Confiteor* after having witnessed his confession. Because of the simultaneous chanting of the schola, the psalm "Judica" and the *Confiteor* were reduced, in people's experience, to a decorative murmuring, so no one was particularly upset when these prayers were struck out. That was wrong, of course. If a prayer has been marginalized, one does not do it justice by dropping it altogether or simply leaving it on the margins; it should be brought back into the center.

The same applies to the Last Gospel. When Holy Mass is celebrated according to the traditional rite, in most cases the priest reads the Last Gospel silently, genuflecting at the "Et Verbum caro factum est" as if it were a private devotion, while the congregation is occupied singing something entirely different. However, the Last Gospel is an additional blessing with the Word; it is a sacramental, for the benefit of the congregation. What better summing-up of the Catholic doctrine of Holy Mass could there be than these concluding words, honored by a genuflection? At the elevation of the Host, we believers have witnessed the Incarnation of the Word; we have seen his glory, sacrificed and transfigured, defenseless and holy. If we feel the need to hold on to this monumental text, we must not treat it as a hastily muttered appendage. As I have already suggested: only if, with quiet concentration, we put the Last Gospel at the very center, shall we secure its essential place in the liturgy.

The rubrics in the 1962 Missal still stipulate that altar servers should reverently kiss every object they hand to the priest, afterward kissing the priest's hand similarly. I can think of no better way of bringing to mind Jesus' "holy and venerable hands"—as the Canon puts it—than this reverent kissing of the priest's hands. It takes place at the very moments when the priest acts out in gestures what he is saying in words, thus expressing that fact that he is now acting *in persona Christi*. In Germany this kissing of the hands is rarely seen, even in traditional circles. People tell me that the custom had died out a long time ago. As for me, I do not know what the custom was. For twenty-five years now "the custom" has been this, that, and everything, and my memory of what went on before that is full of gaps. I take up the old Missal as if I had found it on some deserted beach. I open it and enter into its rich and ordered life, full of meaning. Here is the standard. Compared to this, the regional customs, with the reasons for them—no doubt venerable and serious—have long fallen into shadow.

Entering into the sacred space of the liturgy, every interruption makes me suffer; I suffer whenever the garment of the liturgy is rent (to put it metaphorically). One such rent is the sermon. Let me remind readers what the faithful have experienced prior to the sermon. At the beginning came the entrance procession. The priest, accompanied by the incense and candles that betoken the presence of Christ the King, has approached the altar as a second Christ, as Christ entering into the city of Jerusalem. There, bowing profoundly, he has confessed his sins and summoned the hierarchies of angels and saints, as well as the assembled congregation, to pray for him, and he has imparted to the penitent congregation the sacramental "Indulgentiam, absolutionem". He has incensed the altar, as the body of the dead Christ was treated with spices, thus showing that the altar is Christ. He has sung the *Gloria*, the hymn recalling the presence of the angels who surround the Lord here present. The readings from Holy Scripture have been sung with great solemnity; Christ, speaking in them, has again been honored with a procession, with incense and candles. At this stage the believer is deep in another world. He has understood that all whimsy and spontaneity must be silent when it comes to making visible what is objectively "entirely other". He sees that the celebrant has surrendered his personality to take on a far greater role—and more than a role: he has taken on objective embodiment. The priest's face is seldom seen, for when he briefly turns to the congregation with his greeting "Dominus vobiscum", he keeps his head slightly bowed. It is the Crucified, towering over the altar, who looks at those praying; he is the one who is acting, while his sufferings are recalled, in the tradition's authentic formulae, to the minds of the participants.

Then comes the rupture: the celebrant steps out of this whole sequence, back into his own personality; he is once again the Reverend Father So-and-so. First he reads the notices for the week. "On Monday, Feast of Saint X, Holy Mass at 7 A.M.; Women's Meeting in the afternoon with a slide-show of Baroque churches in Upper Swabia, contributions welcome toward the refreshments." Then he crosses himself and starts to give an explanation of the Scripture. I know as well as anyone else that in the time of Jesus this used to take place in the synagogue, after the readings; and that in the early Church it used to take place at this point, too. Then, however, evidently, the two worlds—the solemn and sacral and the prosaic—were still all of a piece; they fitted into each other, and each operated in a kind of freedom. We can see, for instance, how, in Gregorian chant, the prose of the Bible, the theological speech of Saint Paul, can become song. In the founding era of our faith the different formal genres were not strictly distinguished—the sign of a momentous hour in history. Now, however, a great deal of time has passed. Now, when the sermon begins, I feel as if the supratemporal world I have just entered has suddenly faded. Sobered, I find myself back in my own pragmatic, present-day reality, with all its weakness and half-heartedness. There is no aesthetic solution to this problem. Which inflicts greater damage on the liturgy's unity: the unctuous or brash sermon, the intellectual or hellfire sermon, the fine art or the woodcut, the hearty or the jejune? Everyone is familiar with Bertolt Brecht's theory of epic theatre, an art form that—thank goodness—has long since faded away, suffocated in its own dust. Brecht wanted to promote a rationalistic "Enlightenment"; his plays were not supposed to operate through stage illusion; instead, he wanted to teach the audience by means of transparent parables. The actors had constantly to remind the audience that they (the actors) *were not* the roles they were playing. Brecht was very well acquainted with our old Western culture. I wonder if, in developing his epic theatre, he had in mind the sermon at Mass? It is not totally out of the question. The effect is the same: here the sacrificing priest, too, is shifted back into the context of psychological modernity; the fact that he is "playing a role"—to use the stage language—becomes clear. That would be the case if Holy Mass were a theatrical performance; but the very opposite is true! Through the rites of Holy Mass, in fact, we leave the realm of illusions behind and enter the realm of reality. It is not a question of interruptions in the course of Holy Mass stripping us of illusions; in fact, we are pitched back into the world of illusions at the end of Mass. All the same it is worth pointing out

that the Orthodox Church provides no place for a sermon
during the liturgy: the sermon follows the Mass, after the
priest has taken off his sacred vestments. I can still see a
Russian friend of mine, whom I had taken to a Mass in the
classical rite, shaking his head in disappointment when the
familiar "notices" were read—something that, to Orthodox liturgical sensibilities, is, to say the least, utterly unthinkable. I must make it clear: I am not suggesting that this old
custom of preaching after the Gospel at Mass should be
changed; but I do think it important to realize that there is
a problem here, a "problem" insofar as there is no obvious
solution to hand.

There are two other interruptions of the liturgical flow,
albeit less abrupt than the insertion of the sermon, namely,
the custom of the celebrant withdrawing from the altar and
sitting down to one side while the schola and people sing
the *Gloria* and the *Credo*. I find no directions about this in
the rubrics of the Latin Missal. By leaving the altar in this
way, the priest causes the ceremony to be held up, so to
speak. It is very awkward and again manifests the "two-
track" aspect to which we have already referred. The priest
has read the appropriate prayers quickly and quietly from
the altar card: all that is required has taken place, but the
congregation has still to catch up; it carries on singing slowly
and dragging along, and the priest has to wait until this
obstacle has been finally removed and he may proceed. Moreover, it is the priest's task to put the prayers of the congregation on the altar, as the Archangel Michael does in Saint
John's Apocalypse: if the congregation professes its faith and
so manifests its claim and entitlement to participate in the
mysteries that follow, the priest should receive this profession; he should not read his own prayer and then go off to
one side. Just as we should make all our requests "through

Jesus Christ", liturgical prayer is always made through the priest, as is beautifully clear in the responsories of the major prayers. Take, for instance, the way the *Gloria* and *Credo* are sung antiphonally: Does this not remind one of the way an adult, a mother or father, teaches a poem to a child? A phrase is recited, and the child immediately remembers the rest and can say it. That is how I would like to be led through the *Credo*: like a child being taught by his father, the priest.

If I am right, there are no rubrical objections to the *Gloria* and *Credo* being prayed in common in this way. This encourages me to hope that what I am suggesting is within the realm of what is permissible. What I would like to avoid at all costs is anything resembling the over-busy work of the countless liturgy committees. It is not a question of "shaping" liturgy, as people say nowadays. The miracle is that the liturgy is already there, fully formed, in the rubrics and Mass texts; all we need to do is remove the few things that veil it, to reveal a form that has all the integrity of a sculpture.

Ever since the Reformation great mystical guides of souls have repeatedly urged us to sanctify our everyday lives. It is a sublime goal. Doubtless, the monks' way of life is best disposed to approach such a goal. While I have the greatest respect for this particular spiritual movement, I must point out that striving for this goal can only be the second step in someone's religious life. The first step is seeing the sacred and keeping it sacred, reserving a time and a place, in our everyday lives, for the sacred; the first step is to separate the sacred from the profane. As the Third Commandment puts it: Remember to keep holy the Sabbath day. In the great, ancient liturgy, we observe this Commandment when, on Sunday, the day of the Resurrection, we celebrate the sacrifice that Christ has given us; what we celebrate is not something everyday and ordinary, not the product of human will, but the revealed miracle of God's holiness, an image of our redemption, given to us from above through the Church's hands—in the same way that we receive Holy Communion.

I have already spoken of the condescending smile with which many modern clergy would greet what I have said here. Nowadays it seems as if there are two different kinds of human being in the Church; they can no longer communicate with each other, and could not even if there were good will on both sides. Communication depends by no means only on good will; it depends also on a common language. We have lost this common language: on the one hand, we have a woman who wants to pray the Rosary, and, on the other hand, we have a priest who advises her to do "something sensible" instead. The two are no longer able to have a conversation, and this is not only the result of human sin, it is also the expression of a cultural development in the West that has produced the modern, non-religious, rationalistic, metaphysically blind human being. Sociologists of religion have devoted their attention to this phenomenon. They have a name for the kind of man who believes he can make a connection between the macrocosm and the microcosm by means of sacral acts, who sees the material form as a mirror of transcendence, and who lives in the presence of God (or of the gods): such a man is *homo religiosus*. In this sense practically all people were *homines religiosi* until the eighteenth century. We know that this picture has changed in the West, and we are aware of many people (including Christians) who are no longer "religious people" in this sense. Did we manage to sleep through a change in the *Weltgeist*? Are we dinosaurs—in the last stages of extinction? I shall be careful to make no prediction here.

Nor does it matter. *Homo religiosus* cannot jump out of his own skin; it does not matter to him that he is classed with the masses of Africa, Asia, and Latin America and considered backward in the context of industrial, progressive society. At the age of one hundred, Ernst Jünger reminded us that, measured against the duration of human history, the intellectual world of Voltaire lasted hardly more than a second. *Homo religiosus* reckons time in an entirely different way.

3

Does Christianity Need a Liturgy?

First of all I want to take you to a high mountain, a sheer rock perched above the sea, Monte Tiberio on the island of Capri. On its top was the biggest and most beautiful of Emperor Tiberius' villas, the Villa Jovis; from its terraces one could look down on a massive Temple of Minerva that stood on the mainland—and of which not a stone remains. The Villa Jovis has also been plundered right down to its foundations; some beautiful marble floors from the palace have been relocated in the Capri cathedral. The peasants used to burn marble to obtain lime; the marble statues they did not destroy can be seen in the museum. In former centuries Tiberius was regarded as the same kind of demon as Nero—unjustly, no doubt—but it is a fact that Tiberius was in residence here the same year that his procurator, Pilate, permitted the execution of Jesus. In those years an earthquake destroyed the lighthouse of the Villa Jovis. Tradition says that there are underground lines linking this lighthouse (its ruins are still standing) with Golgotha. So it was not surprising that someone had the idea of building a chapel amid the foundations of the ruined palace on the mountaintop, with a little room adjacent that would house a hermit. Nowadays this chapel is open only once a year, on

September 8, the Feast of the Nativity of Mary; in Naples this is one of the main ecclesiastical feasts, under the title of the Madonna di Piedigrotta, and it is the center of a huge, extravagant local festival. On this occasion the little chapel is decorated with festive lights like a fairground stall, its high altar submerged in fresh gladioli, making the oil painting of the Madonna seem even blacker and more soot-encrusted. For the rest of the year mice run around the deserted building and gnaw their way into the sacristy drawers.

In a period in my life when I spent a lot of time in Capri, I was visited once a year by an English priest who lived in Genoa. He was one of those priests who can be identified by their garb and who are now a rare sight, even in the south of Italy. The Capri clergy were even less impressed by the man in the soutane when they heard that he seriously intended celebrating Holy Mass every day, alone; still, they were prepared to accommodate his religious scruples, offering him the opportunity of concelebrating in the cathedral. The English priest was a very practical man; he was no great theologian but had a very clear grasp of what was absolutely necessary and essential. In the end he was given the key to the little chapel in the Villa Jovis—which was remote and did not constitute a threat. He would not upset anyone there. It was late afternoon when we first ascended to that spot, by a long path that rose gently but constantly to the high ground, giving us a wide view of the gulf. The castle on the top simply did not want to be photographed; since last year it had rusted up in the island's high humidity. We were greeted by an air of decay as we opened the door. The tabernacle's metal door stood open. There were a few dusty flower vases on the altar, and a plastic sheet covered the mildewed altar cloth. The candles

had burned right down. Chairs were scattered around hap-
hazardly. The sacristy looked as though it had been left in
a great hurry. Empty bottles, a tawdry chalice of some kind
of copper alloy, mousetraps, electric cables for the annual
illuminations, desiccated flowers, a chair with three legs—
this was the "still life" presented to us. The priest opened
the drawers. They revealed a damp amalgam of altar linen
and albs and a disintegrating Missal covered in mildew. My
parents had just given me an old Missal; I had wanted one
from the time of the Holy Roman Empire, and the one
they gave me was dated 1805—that is, just within the
period—and published in Regensburg. *This* moldering Missal was the same edition, with the same pale, simple, and
affecting copper engravings. There was nothing romantic
about the desolate chapel. It was not Pompeii but a rubbish
dump that had not yet turned to compost. Unpleasant odors
hung in the air; it was a dead place.

My priestly friend indulged in no such reflections. He
had a purpose in mind, and there was no time to lose. He
opened the window, and warm air seeped in. He took a
straw besom from some corner and started sweeping out
the sacristy. He wiped the altar surface clean. He took the
vestments from the drawers, spread them out, and examined them. Aha, one of the albs was clean and in one piece.
He carefully cleaned the chalice. He discovered a bent
crucifix, kissed it, and placed it on the sacristy chest. He
arranged the altar and put the flower vases in a corner of
the sacristy. The chairs were now in an orderly row. The
altar was covered with a new altar cloth. We found two
candles and put them in the tall altar candlesticks. There
was a "people's altar" in imitation wood, with a metal vine
decoration stuck on to it. "That'll make a good credence
table", the priest said, and in a trice we had put it against

the right-hand wall. He found the bell rope, got on the ladder outside, and fastened the rope to the little bell. Now the bane was broken, the crust of sadness scattered. The wind blew through the open church door like the breath that brings an instrument to life. The priest put on a bespattered stole of violet satin, took a mineral water bottle he had brought with him, emptied its contents into a pink plastic pot, and began to pray; adding salt to the water, he blessed it and poured it into the little marble shells beside the entrance. I thought I could hear the stone breathe a sigh as it came to life again. At this stage a creased chasuble made of gold lurex thread was lying ready in the sacristy. I was pulling on the bell rope. The bell made a thin, clattering sound in the evening air, dispersed to all directions by the wind. People began to approach from the far distance, drawn by the bell. By the time the priest emerged from the sacristy, dressed in the creased gold chasuble, there were about twenty women and children on the rows of chairs. The priest bowed before the altar and began to speak: "Introibo ad altare Dei."

Never had the psalm "Judica" at the beginning of Mass seemed to me so clear and so full of life. The verses seemed to apply specifically to what I had just witnessed and experienced. First, we had left the city where this Mass was not allowed to be celebrated: "Quare me repulisti, et quare tristis incedo, dum affligit me inimicus? (Why hast Thou cast me off? And why go I sorrowful whilst the enemy afflicteth me?) Then there was the long path up the mountain to the chapel: "Emitte lucem tuam et veritatem tuam, ipsa me deduxerunt et adduxerunt in montem sanctum tuum et in tabernacula tua" (Send forth Thy light and Thy truth: they have conducted me and brought me unto Thy holy mount, and into Thy tabernacles). Then there was the clearing out

and preparation of the neglected chapel, and these prelim-
inaries now seemed to me not just a banal cleaning oper-
ation, but actually—in a way that was entirely new to
me—part of the liturgy: "Judica me, Deus, et discerne causam
meam de gente non sancta" (Judge me, O God, and dis-
tinguish my cause from the nation that is not holy). It seemed
to me that the priest had carried out this work of *discernere*
by purifying the place of sacrifice, lighting the candles, blessing the water, wiping away the dust, and throwing the
mousetraps into a corner. By cleaning the chapel up and
getting it ready, he was designating the sacred place, divid-
ing the *gens sancta* from the *gens non sancta*. Like Abel or
Noah, he first of all built an altar before he began the sacrifice; like Moses, he appointed the place where the Ark
of the Covenant would rest. His prayer was preceded by
this delimiting, cleansing, preparing. In fact, prayer was
only possible in this kind of delimited and designated space.
The decision to engage in prayer presupposed the crossing
of a boundary; it was necessary to draw this boundary oneself and, crossing it, leave the unholy people and become a
holy people, a people that could dare to entrust its cause to
God.

At this point I am surprised by a question: What has Christianity got to do with phenomena such as I have just
described? Holy places, the separation of the sacred and the
profane—is this something Christian? I ask this question
with reference to early Christianity and the time of Jesus.
Do we not think of Jesus' activity as a powerful revolution
directed against everything that is ritualistic? Surely it was
the priests and scribes of his day who were most severely
cursed by the Redeemer? We see the twelve-year-old Jesus
teaching in the Temple, in his Father's house, as he himself
says, but when he later returns to the Temple, he does so

for a purpose that has little to do with worship and sacrifice: he invades the Temple, causing mayhem. If we think of the places associated with Jesus' ministry, there is hardly a ritual one among them. Caves, lonely fields, the wilderness, a flat place by the Jordan, various dwelling houses, cattle-watering holes, boat-landing places—these are the settings for his greatest acts. He is a wanderer; around him the old space, the old order seems to be suspended, and the new order he founded is as yet hardly visible. Around him there is no Sabbath, no dietary restrictions, no moral *discernatio*. He enters the houses of the morally untouchable and abruptly dismisses every ritual objection. Where Jesus is, there is cruel want or the most superfluous abandon. When he acts symbolically, that is, in a basically ritual or artistic way, he uses everyday objects. When one reads through the Mosaic dietary regulations, it is amazing to see all the things that could not be eaten, what could not be eaten with what, what must not be consumed hot or cold; compare this with the bread and wine, which were only accompaniments to the Jewish sacrificial meal! He washes the disciples' feet, incidentally giving rise to Christendom's first ritual dispute. Peter clearly understands this act as a kind of baptism and therefore wants to be washed from head to toe, whereas Christ teaches him that this symbolic washing is not an act of the forgiveness of sins, but an expression of the Creator's love for his creatures. The point is that even this washing of the feet is drawn from everyday practice. The Son of Man has nowhere to lay his head; but we clearly sense that he does not want to have such a place; he does not want a holy spot, a divine dwelling, where pious people could erect their tents around him. There is something fortuitous about the great Stations of his suffering—a garden, a courtyard, a street, the place of execution, the grave provided at the last minute. True, they are connected with the city of Jerusalem, but Jerusalem itself is no longer felt to be a holy place: it is a doomed city, handed over to desolation. Even in pre-Christian times Judea was a "holy land"; here, everywhere, the memory of God's deeds through the patriarchs, judges, kings, and prophets was kept alive. Practically all religions cultivate this link with the soil, but Jesus breaks the link with a decidedly sacrilegious unconcern. We can say that, in the ancient world, divinity was very closely connected with particular places. If one wanted to venerate a divinity, one had to visit the place where it resided; leaving this place, one also left its presence. After Constantine, early Christianity conducted a ferocious campaign against the holy places of the old religion. In some ways it is to be regretted. Riotous monks on the loose and mobs whipped up by fanatics torched the temples, throwing down and smashing the ancient images of the gods, which were among mankind's greatest artistic treasures. Paul did not want to hear of any religious feasts being kept. As far as the redeemed were concerned, every day was Easter. Like the Jews in the desert, mankind had been pursuing its pilgrimage through time, but now it had arrived at its goal, and history had come to an end. The baptized lived in an eternal *now*, in the contemplation of Christ. On earth he could only be seen as in a mirror, but the baptized were conscious of being acknowledged and embraced, even now, in the flesh, by their Creator.

There has been a very strong antipathy toward ritual in many phases of Christendom's history. We find it there at its infancy, in Saint Francis of Assisi, in the proto-Protestant movements in the Middle Ages, in the Reformation of Luther and Zwingli, in eighteenth-century Gallicanism and Josephism, and in the liturgical iconoclasm of our day. It seems to me that this anti-ritualism combines with the particular mind-set of the different periods, but at the same time it has very deep roots in Christianity itself. For the most part, the movements that opposed ritual in Christianity were energetic, radical, and passionate; I think that our time presents us with the first example of a liturgical iconoclasm that has come from a religious anemia, an anti-ritualism on the basis of a religion that is feeble.

Every Sunday morning, as a child, I experienced quite a powerful Christian anti-ritualism. It had a profound impression on me. My father was a Protestant, my mother a Catholic. When the church bells rang out, we did not set out for Mass immediately. Not a bit of it. My mother used to wait until she heard the bells ringing for the Gospel—perhaps it was only a single bell—and then she waited a little longer before leaving the house with me, so that she could be sure we would arrive after the sermon. Whenever we went out to church, my father would sit down at his desk and open a little fine-printed Bible. At the back it had a list of the passages appointed for the various Sundays; with a few exceptions they were identical with those in the Catholic Mass. (This ecumenical treasure has been wrecked by the new Lectionary introduced by our so eminently ecumenical reformers.) I can still see him sitting at his little Bible, absorbed in it as if he were the only man in the world. Reading it, he became involved in Jesus' particular milieu, in his space and time. It is consoling for me to see him sitting there. After all, we have no idea how much of the Church's life has been neglected by our bishops in Germany in these last few decades. We could repeat the words of the prophet Daniel: "Iniquity came forth from Babylon, from elders who were judges, who were supposed to govern the people" (Dan 13:5). But there will always be the familiar little black book: it is proof against the destruction. As someone said, "Freedom is alive in second-hand book shops and the photocopier."

We have given a cursory glance at the non-ritual, or decidedly anti-ritual, element in Christianity. We must also ask ourselves this question, however: Is Christian ritual in the Latin, Greek, Coptic, and the many Oriental Churches really something alien to Christianity, something imposed on it, something merely cultural? Could we imagine a Christianity without any ritual, with just the little black book? Or would it not be lacking something essential? Is the Christian ritual we have inherited only the result of rampant "inculturation", as it is now called? We could summarize this view as follows: As it spread out in the Mediterranean lands, the Christian religion—which arose in the poorest and least cultivated corner of the Roman Empire, among primitive and inarticulate people—absorbed everything it found: civilized society, language, philosophy, and art, without worrying about the fact that these forms had arisen in an entirely different world and expressed something quite different. In other words, the link with Jesus Christ could only be established by arbitrary force. What has Jesus Christ to do with Dionysus, the Hellenistic-oriental god of intoxication, whose mystery-cult the Greek Christians could not get out of their minds? What has Mary to do with Isis, apart from superficial features? The Mithras cult, the Imperial court ceremonial, crown and throne, tassels and fringes, ancient rhetoric, the Platonic academy, the Egyptian Serapeum—what has any of this got to do with the Christian religion? Or is there in Christianity, perhaps, something essential that can only be grasped in the form of rite, something that otherwise would be lost?

Some Catholics, who enjoy being provocative, say that the Christian religion could manage without the Bible sooner than without the liturgy. What do they mean by saying this? In the centuries following the Secularization, Jesus attracted much admiration and sympathy from philosophical and philanthropic writers and those in the Enlightenment tradition. Even avowed atheists saw Jesus as a great teacher of humanity, a new Socrates, a new Buddha. "I bow before him as the divine revelation of morality's highest principle", Goethe said to Eckermann. (This dictum should not be used to pigeonhole Goethe as a representative of Enlightenment thought: I quote it only as a particularly clear example of an attitude that has persisted to our time.) Accordingly we read in Goethe's novel *Wilhelm Meisters Wanderjahre*: "Thus, for the noble part of mankind, the way he (Jesus) lived is even more instructive and fruitful than his death." Jesus Christ the Teacher: this is one of the Redeemer's most exalted titles, for Christians too. It was in teaching that he spent the major part of his public ministry. But what was his teaching? Did he proclaim something new? It is obvious, of course, that in religion it is not a case of proclaiming novelties: the subject of religion is not "the new", but "the true". What is true may be ancient, in which case it always remains true; sometimes, if it has been forgotten, it can reappear unexpectedly and so seem to be new. Jesus' truth was an ancient truth; with all his authority he reminded people of what had been revealed in many different ways. The prophets had already taught, and taught impressively, that a man deceives himself if he tries to use sophistry to avoid the divine commands. The commandment of love comes from the Old Testament. The individual petitions in the Our Father come from an ancient tradition of prayer; this only confirms their profound value. Seen as the founder of a religion, Jesus Christ characteristically taught nothing new and certainly no new morality. Nor is this contradicted by the oft-quoted Sermon on the Mount, for it does not deal with moral laws. "Blessed are the poor in spirit—blessed are you who hunger—blessed are you who weep now— blessed are you when men hate you"—these are not moral laws. They are a portrayal and the invocation of a new creation. He who weeps now will laugh—in a new world and once he has "put on Christ", as Paul says. It does not say, "Blessed are the righteous," but "Blessed are those who hunger for righteousness", that is, those who have a sense of the world's fallen-ness and their own failings and who yearn for healing. The restless yearning of which Jesus speaks is not a moral category. It is not something to be achieved by willpower. We cannot desire to be poor in spirit and then hope it will happen. The need to become a new man is not a moral demand. Essentially, morality and holiness are concepts that have hardly anything in common. Of course, this does not mean that one can imagine an immoral saint—although Russian literature, for example, has journeyed far into this territory. No. The only new thing in Christianity, and what distinguishes it from all other religions—what makes it, so to speak, the capstone of all religions—is not the doctrine, but the Person of the God-man, his birth from a Virgin, his sacrificial death for the sins of mankind, his Resurrection from the dead. It is a historical person, not a mythical one, and the historical events of his life can be fairly precisely dated from the reports of the officials of an obscure Roman province. The situation is in fact the very opposite of what Goethe expressed: the teachings of Jesus are less fruitful than his birth, his death, and his Resurrection for mankind—and not merely for the "noble part" of mankind. Only in this context do the teachings of Jesus acquire their authoritative status; otherwise they would be insights of the most sublime wisdom, yet still open to debate. At the center of Christianity, however, stands the miracle of the Incarnation. Only against the background of the Incarnation do all the words and deeds of Jesus exercise their binding claim upon us.

It is this physically embodied God-man who is at the heart of the Christian message. Through the eyes of the Evangelists—in spite of their classically laconic style—we see him not only teaching, but also eating and drinking, feeling hunger, shuddering at the bitter gall offered to him, enjoying the perfume of the jar of ointment, receptive to the beauty of flowers, showing terrible anger, and, most of all, saying nothing. At key points in the Gospel the God-man is silent, or else he does other, strange things that continue to puzzle us: he spits into the dust and makes a dough with it; with his finger he writes words in the sand that no one can decipher; he roasts a fish for his disciples; he sheds tears on learning of the death of Lazarus. We have no idea of his stature and facial features, yet in the Evangelists' accounts we continually see the effect he made on people. The great conversions in the Gospels never come as the result of intellectual battles or instruction, Socratic dialogues, refutation, or persuasion: they happen without a word. Jesus looks at someone eye to eye and binds him to himself forever. He walks down the street, past the beggars and the sick, who find healing through their confession: "I believe". What did the blind and lame "believe" when they saw Jesus walking by? Not the Creed of Constantinople, at all events. Perhaps they could not even have expressed with any clarity what they meant when they said, "I believe". After all, they did not know Jesus at all, nor could they have had any idea of his life story. It was the bodily presence of the God-man, and the certainty that he was there precisely for them, that created in these sick people a union with Jesus. It was this union, far transcending anything they could have known about him, that made them whole.

The early Christians knew that the Christian message was Jesus himself. The essence of the Gospels' new, more profound, and more compelling picture of God was that God had become flesh, present among us, in the God-man. The apostles were clearly aware that they could not hold on to their faith without the physical presence of Jesus, and so, as he left them, Jesus promised that they would never have to do without this presence. "I am with you to the end of days." The promise of the Paraclete is the assurance that the soul's connection with its Creator will not be broken, that God's Spirit is present in his Church; but above all it shows the way in which the physical presence of the Son of God will be continued—in a changed mode—even after he disappears from the visible world; namely, through the action of the Holy Spirit in the liturgy. So began one of the most unique, most magnificent spiritual processes of world history: in order to make present among us the most spontaneous and baffling being in history, personal in the highest degree—the God-man Jesus Christ—a highly restrained, completely harmonious, impersonal, and non-subjective liturgy was created. When we want to identify the action of the Holy Spirit (promised us by Christ) in the Church, we often refer to the presence of the Spirit in the Church's councils and synods and in the grace of state given to bishops and priests, who are illuminated by the Spirit in their doctrinal decisions. I do not want to deny this in the least; but often it is not easy to discern the Holy Spirit's influence with certainty in such cases. We know instances in which the episcopate of an entire country not only took decisions that were dishonorable in the secular sense, but clearly took them in the absence of the Holy Spirit (and of all good spirits). There can be no doubt that the Holy Spirit is only present in the liturgy and the sacraments when he effects the bodily presence of Jesus. Putting it in a nutshell, we could say that Holy Mass is the Holy Spirit promised to the disciples. Jesus, whose physical existence was the core of his message, continues to live physically in the liturgy in the laying-on of hands, in anointing, and in the physical realities of bread and wine.

The early Christians also knew, however, that this presence had to be a gift if it was to be real; that is, it could not be something manufactured, something resulting from man's creativity. Jesus himself had instituted the heart of the rite when he broke bread in the Upper Room of the Last Supper; but it was not simply a case of replaying this scene, because—as the primitive community realized, first gradually and then definitively soon after Jesus' Ascension—the breaking of bread contained not only the event of the Last Supper, but also the sacrifice of Golgotha and the eternal Marriage of the Lamb of which the Apocalypse speaks. If the breaking of bread was a sacrifice, pagan and Jewish sacrificial liturgies could best express it; they were already in existence, and countless people had spoken to God in them. They expressed their waiting for the Redeemer and so were apt to express the Christians' waiting for his return. Those who find fault with the liturgy for retaining elements of ancient paganism would have to apply their criticism with equal severity to the elements of Judaism it contains. When God became man in the Roman colony of Palestine, it was clear that Christianity would have to become a Roman religion, that is, if it were to be, not a Jewish sect, but the Light to lighten the Gentiles, the universal religion. In the Orthodox Church, Socrates and Plato are placed on the same level as the prophets, and on the Areopagus Paul told the Greeks that the God he was proclaiming was the same God of whom their poets had spoken. (No doubt he was thinking of the picture of God presented by Greek tragedy, particularly the tragedies of Sophocles.) Ever since the sacrifice offered by Abel, human history has produced anonymous artistic forms, and now they were filled with the whole depth of the divine presence. Filled in this way, the old forms were naturally transformed into something else. We only have to think of the sacred places, the holy mountains and springs of the pagan and Jewish worlds. Once the period of the persecution of Christians was past and Christianity had become the state religion, pagan sacred places were often chosen when it came to building churches. So temples of Venus became Marian churches, and temples of Mercury became churches of Saint Michael. Nonetheless the "Christian atopia", or "place-lessness", as I call this characteristic freedom with regard to place, asserted itself. Now the place was sacred, not of itself, but because Mass was read there. Furthermore, the place where a church stood was no longer simply this place: it was Jerusalem; nor was it the geographical Jerusalem, but an ideal Jerusalem, that is, heaven. As for the sacrifice that was offered there, it was no longer primarily man's turning to God in the hope of entering into relationship with him through gifts and adoration: it had become God's turning to man. We are constantly being astounded by the reform introduced by Jesus Christ—the only reform that deserves this name. An inherited, sacred form is used to express something completely new, something that reverses all the relationships operating up to that point.

I said that Jesus and his disciples, and the first Christians, were aware that if they were fully to grasp Jesus' message, it was not enough to hand on his teachings faithfully—as, for instance, in the little black book my father used to read on Sundays. If these teachings were to have their effect, it was essential for the disciples to have the experience and know the influence of Jesus, bodily present. And if the liturgy is to be this manifestation of the bodily Jesus, essential for the Christian life, it must be possible to experience it as something that is not a human artifact but something given, something revealed. Thus Basil the Great, a monk and one of the Fathers of the Eastern Church, regarded the Mass as a revelation that is just as great as Holy Scripture, and consequently he strictly forbade anyone to alter or refashion the liturgy. The fact is that the modern reformers of the Mass and the modern exegetes who try to subject revelation to the historico-critical method are birds of a feather. Strangely enough, after all the archaeological and philological expertise, what comes out is a Jesus who could have been an honorary member of the SPD [German Social Democratic Party], a Jesus who is as acceptable to women as Willi Brandt—and equally unresurrected.

Of course we know that the rite has not come down to us unchanged since the days of early Christianity. And yet we can regard the old Mass (wrongly called the Tridentine Mass: it should really be called the Mass of Saint Gregory the Great, just as the Orthodox speak of the Liturgy of Saint John Chrysostom) as something unchanged and unchanging, something that has come down to us directly from heaven. The reason is that these changes were not arbitrary but the result of gradual growth; they took place so slowly that no one really noticed them. The gradual and constant changes that did take place in the rite were not the work of scholars at their desks; they were the result of those praying at Mass over a two-thousand-year history. Only saints such as Ambrose or Augustine or Thomas Aquinas should be allowed to add anything to the Holy Mass, never men at office desks—even if they work in the Vatican. With regard to the question of women priests, a priest said to me: "The idea that women are excluded from the Church's decision making by being denied the priesthood is yet another of the fruits of Modernism, which has brought a tidal wave of decisions into the Church in the areas of theology, liturgy, morals, and law. In former times a priest had no decisions to make. He had to be obedient. A priest had no power, nor does he need to have any." Strictly speaking, this applies to the papacy, too: papal infallibility is nothing other than the pope's submission to revelation and to the teaching of all times.

We know that tradition's mysterious work, making present things that are long past, has been painfully disturbed. Things that are sacral are by definition untouchable, and this untouchability has been gravely damaged; indeed, it is being injured every day, whether by malice or folly. Even among those who will not and cannot abandon the old rite, there is a kind of reforming zeal that can only be attributed to the yearning for self-destruction that sometimes afflicts unsuccessful opposition groups. The highly charged term "pastoral" is always used when liturgical changes are to be introduced. "Pastoral" means pertaining to a shepherd's care, but we have long become used to translating it differently: "We, the clergy, decide how much of the splendor of truth the stupid and confused lay people can take." No one, however, who has found his way, through sacrifice and trials, to the great Christian liturgy will allow any progressive or conservative cleric to deprive him of it. We must not think of the future. The prospects for a liturgical Christianity are poor. From today's perspective, the future model of the Christian religion seems to be that of a North American sect—the most frightful form religion has ever adopted in the world. But the future is of no concern to the Christian. He is responsible for his own life; it is up to him to decide whether he can turn away from the gaze of the liturgical Christ—as long as this Christ is still shown to us.

4

"Tear the Images out of Their Hearts"

Liturgy and the Campaign against Images

At a first glance, what happened to Saint Raphael's church in the Heidelberg suburb of Neuenheim may seem banal enough. The church itself was never at the cutting-edge of Germany's spiritual and intellectual history, nor did it arise out of one of the great periods of architecture, and the architects and artists who collaborated in the building of it are largely unknown. On the other hand, what took place there is typical of what went on in thousands of churches worldwide, whether they were artistic masterpieces or anonymous productions, cathedrals or chapels. Hardly a single church was left untouched in the wake of Vatican II, and if, after all, one *does* come across an unscathed architectural ensemble, it is not because reverence or taste has spread its protecting wings over it: it is probably due to a lack of money—a lamentably rare occurrence in a country where the population pay church tax. No German bishop can deny that something similar to what happened to Saint Raphael's took place frequently in his diocese. These are the spiritual and liturgical fruits of the postconciliar development. Anyone who wants to see, embodied, the horrors implied in the volatile concept of *aggiornamento* should take a look at the short, revealing history of Saint Raphael's.

I used the word "banal" in connection with the Neuenheim church. Can there be such a thing as a banal church? According to secular artistic categories, perhaps, and if we adopt a strictly scientific standpoint that excludes any reference to the function of the object in question. But if we ask who commissioned this (or any) church, the answer must be: the liturgy. Often, indeed, the liturgy created a magnificent frame, decorated with eloquent and significant forms, in which it could unfold its life. A church that is to house a consecrated Host, the Blessed Sacrament, cannot be banal. Of course there are churches that clearly proclaim what they are for and others that do so less clearly or not at all. It is also true that the liturgy is fundamentally independent of the spatial conditions under which it is carried out. Yet the observer may be forgiven for drawing conclusions, on the basis of a church's outward appearance, about the liturgy that is celebrated in it; faced with an ecclesial space that no longer speaks of sacral and liturgical functions, one may well ask whether it is a fit place for the celebration of the liturgy.

When the foundation stone for Saint Raphael's church was laid in 1903, the priest and community shared the conviction that they were building a church that should be immediately recognizable as such to everyone who saw it. At that time, in fact, people were no longer building in the neo-Gothic style, which meant that the design produced by the diocesan architect Ludwig Maier was already a little old-fashioned. Maier was an experienced professional. His edifice is fine, well-proportioned. One can see that he was influenced by the façade of Pisa Cathedral, but the bright brickwork also recalls Maier's contemporary milieu, the industrial architecture of the factories—those monuments of an era, now rightly protected as such. There is something cold about the atmosphere in Saint Raphael's; it has this in common with many other buildings inspired by historical precedents. This coldness is a feature of the industrial century, and in Bauhaus architecture it is even prized as a positive quality. In its delicate compactness Saint Raphael's resembles the kind of reliquary one sees in the form of a church—it is a model church. Maier richly decorated the interior. He was not concerned about purity of style: he was aiming at a new style, produced on the basis of the fullness of the Christian past and illustrating the Church's journey through history. Early Christian mosaics from Roman basilicas, the Byzantine art of Ravenna, the Italian Renaissance, the Baroque of the Counter-Reformation, Sacred Heart spirituality, and the cult of the saints—all these combined to give a really astonishing compendium, in painting and sculpture, of the Catholic religion. Explaining to a child the windows, frescoes, and altars of Saint Raphael's, one could communicate a great sense of the Church's faith and history.

Today we can only guess what impression the church would have made at the time, with its multi-colored splendor and its paintings; the few remaining photographs give no idea of the colors or the execution. From contemporary sources, however, we know that the artifacts were precisely related to one another. The great prayers, the Stations of the Cross and the Litany of Loreto, adorned the walls and the coffered ceiling, as if the sacred space itself were fashioned out of prayer.

All this was being created in the same years that Kandinsky was painting his first abstract watercolor. In the realm of art a great civil war broke out, and it has lasted right down to the present day. This is not the place to go into the development of art in the twentieth century; suffice it to say that there is still great realistic art in the twentieth century, but it is hardly visible. Everything that had been significant since the dawn of art, namely, the study and the artistic re-creation of the world, was now outlawed. Prior to this revolution, art, particularly in its most sublime works, had always fulfilled a function: it had ennobled a space or preserved someone's memory. Artists painted church walls with the *biblia pauperum* and created devotional images that gave a specific direction to prayer.

Modern art, celebrating its triumph, uttered its own *non serviam*. No longer would it serve. It demanded for itself the reverence—undiminished—that heretofore had been directed to its subject matter. The Church should long have been aware that the art she had fostered in her own bosom was trying to free itself from its mother. Revolutions do not happen overnight; they require preparation. For some time the Church had no longer been art's greatest patron, and art goes where the bread is. For too long the Church had been in a timorous and defensive position and could no longer attract free spirits. What had already happened in philosophy and society had to be taken account of in the world of art; the Church had lost her power and influence.

The destruction that took place in the Second World War cut the Gordian knot, facilitating decisive action. A bomb had blown out a number of Saint Raphael's windows; in 1954, while the scaffolding was still in place, the opportunity was taken to paint the whole church white. Abstraction—in the form of this covering of snow— descended on the wealth of forms of the *communio sanctorum*.

The church's most precious treasures, the high altar and side altars, were still intact. These altars, from the studio of the Sigmaringen wood sculptor Alfons Marmon, were notable works of art that exhibited the independence and theological daring characteristic of great church art. (An examination of the role played by painters and sculptors in the development of the Church's teaching office would produce some surprising results.) Although art historians have subsequently rehabilitated historicism, people often continue to criticize nineteenth-century buildings for their imitation, lack of originality, and eclecticism. This flies in the face of the evidence: the unprejudiced observer will see immediately that these works of art, precisely by playing with the tradition as they did, produced completely novel forms. And if the art historian actually does notice these new forms, the artist—in this case, Alfons Marmon—is attacked for producing an altar that is not Romanesque.

Marmon's altars were, indeed, not Romanesque, not least because this kind of high altar was unknown in the Romanesque period. Its triumphal arch comes from the Florentine Renaissance. The Della Robbia family has given us examples of these altars in deep relief. Marmon's lime-wood sculptures hold a superlatively artistic balance between the observation of nature, on the one hand, and a stylized execution, on the other: we see large, nervous hands and spiritual heads, surrounded by flowing garments in *Jugendstil*. It is worth spending time to appreciate the entire conception of the altar. Its theme is the Incarnation. The gates to the right and left of the tabernacle led into the Casa Santa of Nazareth and the Nativity grotto of Bethlehem, the two places associated with the Incarnation of the Word. On the altar of the historical Casa Santa, today in Loreto, we read in letters of bronze: "Hic verbum caro factum est"—here the Word was made flesh. This has a twofold reference, for Mary bore Jesus within the walls of this house, and an Incarnation likewise takes place on the altar at Mass.

By carving both Annunciation and Nativity on his altar, Marmon was emphasizing this aspect of the Mass, shifting the accent from the sacrifice to the sacrificial gift, the God-man. The message of this altar was that Christ was not only sacrificed on the altar: he was also born on it.

Compared with the Byzantine icons, few of the images produced by the Latin Church have the same theological force and bodily conviction. Characteristically, most of the Latin images were created as a result of visions: the Pietà, the Mother of God absorbed in contemplation of her dead Son, comes from the mysticism of Thuringia; the Immaculata of Lourdes comes from the apparitions to Bernadette, and the Sacred Heart image comes from the visions of Margaret Mary Alacoque. The image of the Sacred Heart is the most eloquent representation of the mystery of the God-man. The body in which this mystery is brought about is manifested in a burning Heart, a blood-red internal organ emitting flames of divine love. Below the arch of his Sacred Heart altar Alfons Marmon placed an image of Christ as the Sacred Heart, but it is not addressed to the individual's intimate devotion: here Christ is the Pantokrator. This combination of the divine Ruler of the World and the Sacred Heart of Jesus was, perhaps, a unique achievement; it contains a theological truth of inexhaustible depth. Marmon also found unusual themes for the side altars; there was Saint Charles Borromeo giving Communion to Saint Aloysius Gonzaga. Gerhard Tersteegen writes that the true history of the Church is the history of the saints—the rest can be safely allotted to profane history; I have seldom found this thought so forcefully expressed as on this altar.

The liturgy constructs its own space, its own ambience. This is equally true in the case of the Mass of Paul VI. In 1968 the parish of Saint Raphael (still numbering some of the original benefactors of the altars in its ranks) was told that Marmon's altars were "controversial". Note the date: 1968 was an "axis" year in Karl Jaspers' sense: there were student riots in Germany, France, and the United States; it was the beginning of the Chinese "cultural revolution", with its millions of victims, its full-scale attack on images, and its destruction of temples and art treasures—and it was the year of the liturgical reform. These events are connected, even if they do not seem to be. Future historiography will have no choice but to see a profound link here. In Neuenheim's Saint Raphael's church, however, the upheavals did not take place in a revolutionary manner. The parish priest was also parish priest of Heidelberg city. He was reputed to have "masterfully carried out the various changes in the intellectual and spiritual life in the Church and in the external reordering of church buildings in the wake of the Council". At the celebrations for the fiftieth anniversary of his priestly ordination, he was praised for having "carefully prepared the community for the change"; like an experienced surgeon, he did this preparatory work before making the quick and radical incision. It had been said that the Marmon altar was of plaster; this was clearly proved to be untrue when the sculptures were chopped and sawn to pieces, revealing the lime timber beneath the painted surface. Photographs show the venerable old priest in his utterly correct clerical garb, not looking at all like an agent of vandalism, smiling serenely as he observed the results of his destruction.

How was this possible?

I was born after the Second World War, in 1951. As a child I remember older people coming to the house, white-haired intellectuals, the men with what we called "Caesar" haircuts and the women with ponytails; they wore crude amber necklaces over their sackcloth garments. For me, the "modern" style has always borne an old face. These people were marked by the experience of the youth movement before the First World War. It was the crucible of the century's ideas. Political movements that were to become deadly enemies sponsored the youth movement—one only has to think of Communism and National Socialism. The youth movement fed the roots, not only of the cult of nudity, feminism, vegetarianism, neo-paganism, pseudo-Indian meditation, gay liberation, ubiquitous guitar-strumming, and the Bauhaus: it was also behind the liturgical reform. Basically all these movements can be traced back to the burning idealism of good people who were led astray and betrayed; but that subject must be left to another time. However, the delight in destruction that was once conjured by young people, their cheeks aglow in the light of the campfire as they talked and sang of their vision—the collapse of the old system and the advent of a wondrous new age—outlived its infantile phase and achieved an astonishingly advanced age. As Goethe's Mephistopheles wryly says of the enthusiastic young *baccalaureus*, "This heady juice, absurd and immature / Will one day yield a goodly wine, I'm sure." Goethe could not have guessed, however, that in the twentieth century people would find a way to stop the fermentation process. Now, in a false youthfulness, the "heady juice" retains its sweetness forever, producing a fatal brew that only gives headaches and cannot be called real "wine". The twentieth-century cult of youth culminates in a cruel curse: while the aging process cannot be stopped, the aging human being is not allowed to mature and is condemned, until his life's end, to play the long-dead games of his youth. This is most clearly seen in the world of art—which is so closely related to religion—where the avantgardisms of 1905 are still being repeated again and again, as an ossified ritual, a hundred years later. And, with her famous *aggiornamento*, the Church thinks that, in order to survive, she needs to "open herself" to these senile avantgardisms!

Back to the story of Saint Raphael's in Neuenheim. The apse alone was completely cleared out. In the celebratory pamphlet for the parish priest's jubilee we read that "the remodeling is harmonious, even elegant". "The table-altar is designed for the New Covenant community meal. . . . No communion rails impede the access of the faithful. The priest presides, as is appropriate, over the eucharistic community; . . . he is the president of the community, he leads the assembly"—indeed he does, from the very place where, formerly, the tabernacle stood. The latter, in the form of a bifurcated bronze tooth, has been relegated to a little cupboard in a side wall. "It is simply a case of a slight shift in the scale of values", the parish priest told the congregation. "Now, in the foreground stands the action of the meal and the active participation of the mature Christian." Yes, indeed, the scale of values has shifted somewhat. What did the disciples' "active participation" consist of in the Upper Room, when they let Christ wash their feet? What was the "active participation" of Mary and John as they stood beneath the Cross? It consisted of beholding, letting it happen, watching and praying. However, I will not waste time on a critique of the jargon of the "reform", which has already been frequently and thoroughly exposed for what it is. Like Moses, the town parish priest was not permitted to enter the Promised Land. He led his parish out into the white steppe. It was for the next generation to fill in the empty space.

Along with the youth movement came the handicraft and do-it-yourself movement; it became a philosophically and intellectually respectable activity and approach. Artists of the avant-garde practiced this shaman's craft of sticking and hammering together all kinds of rubbish and endowing the resulting phantasmagoria with profound significance. As the Christian priesthood was being demolished, a new caste of art-priests was forming, laying their hand in blessing on absolutely anything and announcing it to be a "work". Otto von Simson, who was really very well acquainted with medieval painting, discovered that two empty plastic blood plasma bottles that Joseph Beuys had mounted beside a broken stick (the work was called *Crucifixion*) showed "the power of a Giotto". If this was taking place in the lofty world of art criticism, one can hardly find fault with the parish priest of Saint Raphael's for commissioning a priest friend of his—a DIY rubbish-artist in Beuys' style and an art-priest in both senses—to produce a Crucifixion for the empty apse. This was needed, for they had no cross; nor, of course, was there one on the altar. Once again the congregation was "carefully" prepared. As an official of the Catholic Academy in Mainz suggested: "People who expect the Stations of the Cross to be 'beautiful' should be looking for them in neat garden allotments, not on Golgotha." So much for Cimabue, Botticelli, Tintoretto, and Raphael, who dared to show the transcendent, indestructible beauty of the God-man shining even through his sufferings! And note the entirely typical scorn for the concerns and occupations of ordinary folk! Catholic officials may, indeed, be far above the world of garden allotments; but tending such a garden is a humane and worthy occupation—and has far more point to it than attending discussion evenings at the Catholic Academy. Liturgical art has to minister to allotment gardeners, too. The miracle of Catholicism was a rite that spoke to mankind's most elevated minds and to unlettered goat-herds, to Chinese and Africans, Crusader knights and atomic physicists.

When the Marmon altars were destroyed, the dismayed and confused congregation was silent; they had been trained to trust and obey their shepherd. There was resistance, however, when the parish priest tried to persuade them to fund the acquisition of a collage by the priest and artist Udo Körner. The work was called *Schrei und Wolke* [Cry and cloud]. The body of the Crucified is of tree bark; it is only suggested. There is no identifiable mouth that might utter a cry. Both cross and body are split—not, no doubt, to recall the chopping-up of the Marmon altar. Rusty wire netting hangs in the darkness above the cross. Körner's idea—one of a million ideas of this ilk—was to "disturb pious ways of viewing things". In the aesthetic debate, people are always mistakenly drawing up battle lines—as if the celebrated *Stag at Bay* were being confronted by an oh-so-courageous little band of the avant-garde. But there *is* no *Stag at Bay* any more. Nowadays its place is taken by works like *Schrei und Wolke*, the kind of art that "shakes things up, asking penetrating questions of unvarnished honesty"—as the tired phrase is trotted out. Still, the debate about whether to buy *Schrei und Wolke* for the apse in Saint Raphael's did lead to something good. The work now hangs, in fact, where the Marmon altar used to stand; but a senior member of the parish said something that made the whole battle worthwhile, a fundamental principle of really great simplicity: "Christ took flesh and became man: shouldn't he be portrayed as a human being?"

"They hack and chop as if they were in a wood or a forest, indiscriminately destroying altars and paintings." So complained Martin Luther, hearing of the excesses of iconoclasm prompted by the inflammatory sermons of his former protégé Andreas Bodenstein of Carlstadt. Luther, however, was not without blame for the iconoclasm of 1521 and 1522, which was followed by many more such instances on the part of Calvinists. He was horrified when he realized what his writings had done. We can see what the smashing of images meant from a contemporary report of the destruction of the monastery of Reinhardtsbrunn, the burial place of the Landgrave of Thuringia:

> The most wanton malice was vented on the monastery. With sacrilegious hands, the rabid people smashed all twenty-three altars with their precious carvings, sculpture, and holy images, because they were objects of the Catholic veneration of saints; they threw them into the fire, tearing and cutting up the precious altar coverings; they smashed the three organs and the twelve bells, sharing among themselves anything they might find useful. They emptied the holy oil of consecration from its beautiful jug and poured it on the ground and scattered the Hosts of the Blessed Sacrament. In their frenzy they tore the saints from their niches and stamped on them.

This was followed by the desecration of tombs and a great burning of books: the monastery's entire handwritten library went up in flames. No: this work of destruction was not carried out in a "harmonious, even elegant" manner, nor was anyone "carefully" prepared for it. The work of destruction carried out in the wake of the Second Vatican Council differs here from the Reformation iconoclasm, although there are similarities.

All the same, what we have gone through in the last thirty-five years *is* an iconoclasm. These decades were characterized by both the destruction of images and an inability to create images. The new altar image of Saint Raphael's is only superficially an image: in reality it is the rejection of all image.

A question arises here: How could liturgical images of the God-man be produced in an age when the prevailing tendency in art rejects the depiction of human beings altogether? Would it not be easier and more convenient to retreat to the Second Commandment—"You shall not make for yourself a graven image"? Both Byzantine and Reformation iconoclasm interpreted the Commandment in this way. The Church was accused of flying in the face of this divine injunction on Mount Sinai by engaging in the cult of icons and the images of saints. This was indeed a terrible accusation, for who could dare to infringe a divine command? The accusation also explains the frenzy of destruction wreaked upon images in Byzantium and during the Reformation; people saw it as a holy rage, and this, perhaps, shows the greatest difference between it and the current iconoclasm, where images are destroyed out of *angst* and pusillanimity.

Was the Church mistaken when, in the Catacombs, she became a Church of images? The Second Commandment is unambiguous. Only God can revoke it. And God has revoked it. He created his own likeness. We could even go so far as to call Jesus Christ God's self-portrait, for, if anyone, after Adam, was God's likeness, it was Jesus. Ever since the coming of Jesus Christ, the Second Commandment is: "You shall have for yourselves an image of God, and this image is Jesus Christ."

This image, then, is totally different from the magnificent depictions of the mythical gods. It belongs to an entirely different artistic genre. We have mentioned the term "portrait": the image of Jesus belongs to the portrait genre; it is the portrait of a real person. At the time of the early Christians the art of portraiture was highly developed. At that time in Fayum, in Hellenistic Egypt, we find portraits that are the most realistic depictions of human beings, and Rome at the same time saw a blossoming of the art of the bust-portrait. People knew what a portrait was. Naturally, too, Christ was not to be idealized like a Greek god. Nor was this necessary, because the early Christians possessed a real portrait, the impression left on the great linen cloth that was held to be the cloth that was found, folded up, in the empty tomb, as is mentioned in John's Gospel. This cloth served as a model for the early icon painters of Christ. The unique face on this cloth became a standard for images of Christ. It was modified over the centuries, particularly in the West, but remained recognizable to everyone until the most recent past and could still be seen in the Sacred Heart depiction found on the Marmon altar. The way the master painters treated the image of Christ at a time when painting was beginning to separate itself from religion is highly revealing: for instance, Veronese's paintings of the Last Supper and the Wedding of Cana show Christ among a lively crowd of people, but Christ himself seems strangely pale because the painter did not dare (nor was it permissible) to depart from the tradition when representing Christ. Artists who knew nothing of the grave cloth nonetheless held to the traditional model. Something similar applies to the images of the Mother of God; the main issue is not whether the Evangelist Luke really painted Mary's portrait; it is that the early Christians wanted to have a real image of Mary and not a fictitious one.

Christ is the Truth. We need to behold this truth, for it transcends all knowledge (to quote a phrase of Gregory of Nyssa), and that is why what the Reformation called the "worship of images" is in fact an essential element in the Christian religion. Christians cannot venerate sacred images enough, for they are reflections (albeit pale ones) of the Incarnation. Even the most clumsy image is like the hem of Jesus' garment that was seized by the woman in the crowd "because a power went out from him", as we read in the Gospel of Luke, the painter of the Madonna. It is one of history's most remarkable coincidences that, at the beginning of this century, when people were losing the ability to paint human beings, photographic negatives brought the body on the Turin Shroud back into general awareness, so that the image of the God-man should not vanish in the cultural catastrophe of the "loss of the image".

Just as the image of Christ was chosen by God himself, and just as Christians endeavored to hold on to this real picture, they also linked the liturgy, which is itself a great image—which is why the crisis affecting holy images goes hand in hand with the liturgical crisis—very closely with the concrete places associated with our salvation. In the earliest times Mass was celebrated in the Holy Grave, where the folded cloth was found, because Christians knew that the Eucharist is primarily a representation, not of the Last Supper on Holy Thursday, but of the Lord's death and Resurrection. Today, in the church of the Holy Sepulchre in Jerusalem, one can still see how the grave's local specifics created the great liturgy. I am referring, not to the church building that houses the grave, but to the narrow grave chambers, the anteroom where the women saw the young man in radiant white clothing, and the actual grave chamber itself, with its niche for the body. Only very few people can be present at a Mass celebrated there. The priest stays with the people in the anteroom until the Creed. For the sacrificial part of the Mass, he enters the grave chamber. There he is alone and invisible. The altar is the niche in which the body of Jesus lay. The white altar cloth is the shroud, and the Host is the body. The way in which the Host is filled with the life of the Godhead remains hidden from the congregation, which only hears the whispering of the priest. The Sacrifice of the Mass and the Resurrection become one. At the same time it becomes clear why the early Christians wanted the holy mysteries to take place behind the iconostasis, the choir enclosure, the altar rails, obscured by the priest's body. The hermetic aspect, the aspect of rapture, that surrounds the Consecration even in the old Latin liturgy, represents nothing other than the Holy Sepulchre, shut with a stone, in which the God-man awoke from death. This event had the whole cosmos for its witness, but no living man saw it. Something that, in the liturgy, seems to be a later accretion, an accompaniment found in Byzantine basilicas and Gothic cathedrals, thus proves to be intimately connected with the core of salvation history. Christian liturgy is a waiting beneath the Cross and outside the grave. This is another image the liturgical reform has tried to erase.

The Jerusalem grave is the image of the old liturgy. It looked toward the Risen One and so faced east. For the old liturgy, the rising sun was a sign of the creation of the world, of the Resurrection, and of the Second Coming of Christ. Priest and people faced in the same direction, united in prayer and expectation. In the wake of the liturgical reform, the priest turned around and now looks at the congregation while pretending to be speaking to God. The model for the new liturgy is the committee table at a party or club meeting, with microphone and documents; on the left an ikebana dish with dried flowers and a bizarre orange-colored exotic plant, and on the right a couple of TV candles in hand-thrown pottery holders. Serious and recollected, the committee members look at the public, just like priests at a concelebration. The club meeting with its democratic order of business is the phenotype of the new liturgy; this is utterly logical, for those who reject the supratemporal mystery are bound to end up in the socio-political reality. There is no third way. From time to time, of course, the public face breaks down. Some clerics, it is said, have difficulties putting on the right face when it comes to the Consecration. What is the appropriate facial expression at the Consecration? This suggests another Goethe quotation from the dialogue between Faust and Wagner: "Oft have I heard it said / An actor might instruct a parson. —If the parson's an actor, yes, / As comes about from time to time." Thus, logically, the ancient Mass texts for the Feast of the Martyrs Perpetua and Felicity have been cut out, since they made reference to "blessed secrets" and "mysterious gifts and delights". Clearly, no one can expect to hear of "mysterious gifts and delights" from a committee podium.

When a rite is no longer recognized as having the power to make Incarnation present, even those parts of the Mass that do not seem to be primarily ritual—such as the Gospel and the Creed—are no longer understood in the fullness they have in the liturgy. What is liturgical? We could say that "liturgical" means effective and operant prayer. Liturgical prayer is always sacramental: it effects the sanctifying and grace-giving action of Christ. So the reading of the Gospel at Mass is not the communication of a text for the listeners to grapple with: it is the presence of Christ, teaching, healing, and forgiving sins. Moreover, the Gospels seem to be written with this in mind. The Creed, too, considered as a liturgical prayer, is not a collection of dogmas that were defined at various councils (and some of which were imposed by main force) but a means whereby the individual plunges once again into the purifying freshness of baptism, the presence of the communion of saints, the Church-creating power of the Holy Trinity. There is no question of this kind of efficacy in the new liturgy, nor is it intended.

It is characteristic of this century that just as the axe was being applied to the green tree of liturgy, the most profound insights into liturgy were being formulated, albeit not in the Roman Church but in the Byzantine Church. On the one hand, a pope dared to interfere with the liturgy. On the other, Orthodoxy, separated from the pope by schism, preserved the liturgy and liturgical theology through the terrible trials of the century. For a Catholic who refuses to accept the cynic's easy conclusions, these facts produce a baffling riddle. One is tempted to speak of a tragic mystery, although the word tragic does not fit in a Christian context. The Mass of Saint Gregory the Great, the old Latin liturgy, now finds itself on the "lunatic fringe" of the Roman Church, whereas the Divine Liturgy of Saint John Chrysostom is alive in all its splendor in the very heart of the Orthodox Church. The idea that we have something to learn from Orthodoxy is not a popular one. But we must accustom ourselves to studying—and studying thoroughly— what the Byzantine Church has to say about sacred images and the liturgy. This is equally relevant to the Latin Rite; in fact, it seems as though we can only get to know the Latin Rite in all its Spirit-filled reality if we view it from the Eastern perspective. The greatest liturgical writer of our century was the Russian priest Pavel Florensky, who was shot under Stalin's regime in 1938. He is not a saint of the Orthodox Church, nor is his canonization in view, but I regard it as one of the greatest signs of hope that Pope John Paul II installed Florensky's picture in his private chapel.

Chesterton reminds us that a hope that is based on the least probability cannot actually be described as a Christian virtue. So while it may be naïve to hope that a pope who reads Florensky might revitalize the ancient Christian liturgy, there is still plenty of room for a great and absurd Christian hope of this kind. Anyone who believes that the liturgy of the Incarnation and sacred images are intimately and essentially linked to faith in Christ—and actually come forth from him—anyone who finds it easier to imagine the total collapse of religion than its continuance in the absence of liturgy, can be quietly confident about the outcome of the present catastrophe. As the example of Byzantine iconoclasm shows us, a hundred years is a relatively short time to overcome this kind of sickness. Until this happens what we need, as was shown in the resistance offered by the Byzantine Church, is utterly resolute priests and monks to keep the tradition alive, so that it will not have to be reconstructed from books in some future time. When the destruction of the altars took place in Saint Raphael's in Heidelberg, many of the parishioners rescued items and brought them home with them. They could follow the example of Saint Francis in rebuilding the Portiuncula chapel and try to reconstruct the Sacred Heart/Pantocrator altar. On the first Sunday of Lent the Orthodox Church celebrates the end of iconoclasm with the great "Feast of the Reestablishment of Orthodoxy". So it is my dream that, one day, when this altar and many other high altars are reerected, we shall be able to give thanks as we celebrate the reestablishment of Latin Orthodoxy.

5

Tradition's Avant-Garde

The Benedictines of Fontgombault

The wide stone quadrangle is paved with huge, irregular slabs that are apt to trip up the unwary. Two young men are walking along it; they are wearing black leather jackets, and their hair is cropped short. They are cadets from some military academy, in civilian rig. After them comes a rather corpulent elderly man with gold-rimmed glasses and the red ribbon of the *Légion d'honneur* on the lapel of his dark blue jacket. Next comes an old priest in a somewhat bespotted soutane, followed by a small boy in short trousers and legs that are red with the cold. It is so cold that our breath makes white clouds. The little procession comes to a halt beside a small gate in the long wall. We all wait. A young monk dressed in a black habit emerges, carrying a gilded basin and a jug, with a light hand-towel over his arm. The monk keeps his head bowed; it is clear that, in doing this, he is following some regulation.

A gray-haired monk comes to meet the group. He wears a golden cross on a chain upon his breast and holds his hands concealed beneath the scapular, the broad strip of cloth that hangs down back and front. He greets everyone separately;

the guests approach him, going down on their left knee to kiss his golden ring. Then he beckons the monk with the basin and jug. Each guest holds his hands over the basin as the gray-haired monk pours water from the jug and then offers them the towel. The guests pass through the narrow gate and find themselves in a high, bare room with gothic arches. A hundred or so monks are standing there at the rows of refectory tables, their hands hidden under their scapulars. All are silent. So begins the evening meal in the Benedictine monastery of Our Lady of Fontgombault.

If a visitor were to sum up, in a single abstract phrase, the multiplicity of impressions produced by a ritual meal of this kind, he might be inclined to talk about the dissolving of the distinction between what is important and what is not. All the utensils for the meal are used in a deliberate and conscious manner, even if they are neither precious nor even beautiful. The jug and basin that were used by the abbot to wash the guests' hands are now standing in a stone niche, just as, in the abbey church, the water used for washing the priest's hands at Mass is kept ready near the altar. At the end of the meal each monk cleans his spoon and knife with his napkin and wraps them both in the white cloth. In the same way, at Mass, the careful cleansing of the chalice after Holy Communion brings the liturgical actions to an end.

A book is read aloud during the meal. First it is a chapter from the Rule of the Order; but after that the reading is taken from a book on recent French history. This is done from a pulpit, and the text is recited—sung, in fact—in a kind of chant, its secular content notwithstanding. Whenever the monks who serve the meal enter or leave the refectory, they bow before the great crucifix above the abbot's place, which is raised a little above the others; if they have something to say to him, they kneel and whisper into his ear as he inclines toward them. The abbot uses a little wooden hammer as a sign to start the meal, and he gives the same sign for it to end. Similarly, in the great conventual Mass, the master of ceremonies gives similar signs to the celebrants, tapping his prayer book with his knuckle to indicate the next section of the ceremony.

The meal consists of a few radishes in butter, a clear vegetable soup, some grated carrot, a piece of fish in a white sauce, green salad, cheese from the monastery's own dairy, and chicory coffee, all accompanied by a perfectly clear, dry red wine. The dishes reflect the austerity or splendor of the liturgy of the day: on fast days the meals incline to frugality; on feast days they are marked by a hint of elegance. Every day the meals take place in an identical pattern and to the precise minute, yet no one seems inhibited or hurried by this strict formality. An old shoemaker, retained by the monastery to make and repair the monks' shoes, eats his pear and bread in peace and recollection and has just folded up his napkin as the abbot takes up his little hammer.

Although the Abbey of Fontgombault was founded nine hundred years ago, it is a relatively young monastery. After the building of the majestic Romanesque abbey church and centuries of flourishing life came an early decline and the destruction wrought by the wars of religion; increasingly, the life of the monastery became a shadow of its former self under the administration of abbots *in commendam*, who regarded it primarily as a source of income, and it was finally dissolved shortly before the French Revolution. The abbey church was plundered as a source of stone: the choir and west façade remained intact, but the cut stones from the nave can be found in the walls of the surrounding gray farmhouses. In the second half of the nineteenth century the missing parts of the edifice were replaced, albeit in a rather unimaginative way.

Each of the old stones has its distinctive character; they are worn at the edges and shine like polished bone; compared with the new nave, which is all straight lines, the choir's axis inclines gently to one side. In the monastery they say it recalls the head of the crucified Lord, fallen onto his shoulder. As a result of the vicissitudes of history French churches are often very bare. Here, too, the wide cathedral-like building with its three naves contains only one image: Notre-Dame de Bien-Mourir, "Our Lady of a Good Death"—a stone sculpture representing the Mother of God enthroned, her majestically fixed eyes suggesting something of the late Rome of the emperor Constantine.

Not until 1949 did Benedictine monks return to the monastery. The new foundation was made from the Abbey of Solesmes, which in the nineteenth century played a part in the rediscovery of the old Gregorian chant. But it was not until after the Second Vatican Council that the abbey's mysterious fame spread far beyond the borders of France. In a time like ours, so preoccupied with reform, this return to the full Rule of Saint Benedict, to the unabridged Liturgy of the Hours and to the great liturgy of the West—which essentially comes down to us from the time of Pope Gregory the Great (540–604)—is regarded as a reform of a particularly daring kind.

Most of those who travel to Fontgombault are young people. Most of the monks, too, are young. In their habits they look like figures from a Giotto fresco, but when they have visitors they can be seen walking up and down the garden of the guest wing with their brothers and relations who wear modern clothes, and it is quite clear that they are not living in the Middle Ages. The family visit brings out the change that is effected at the clothing of a new monk: his head is shaved, and his body, shown to best advantage by his former civilian garb, disappears under the shapeless black habit. The goal seems to be a maximum of uniformity, yet what results is the very opposite. What initially struck the onlooker as something highly antiquated is now seen to be an individuality heightened by being inserted into timelessness, whereas formerly it had hidden behind the fashionable hairstyle, the multi-colored pullovers and jackets of the up-to-the-minute collective.

At first the visitor may find the Masses and the Gregorian chant an intricate drama, hard to follow. As the day unfolds, however, he discovers in small ways that it is not a drama at all—or rather, that it is a drama that has no end. He discovers that, in this world of the cloister, there is no other life "below the surface"; there is no trivial world with occasional high points of festal ceremony. The Rule of Saint Benedict, and the way it is translated into life in Fontgombault, aims to prevent any part of life from being bracketed out: instead, the whole day is pronounced to be liturgy. Thus, amazingly, liturgy and courteousness become intertwined. Two monks whose paths cross many times in a day bow to each other with the very same gesture that is given to the priest at Mass. When anyone knocks at the door, he hears the reply "Deo gratias!" from inside. Every mundane document and every letter begins with the word "Pax!" As soon as a guest arrives he is conducted to the church, where the monk who received him prays for him in silence. In the quadrangle that joins the church to the refectory, the monks avoid walking on the middle of the path, which is marked by a ribbon of stone; this is reserved for the priest during the procession on feast days. The monks who work in the fields, in the vineyard, or with the cattle are helped to remain in contact with the spiritual life of the monastery by the various bell signals that ring out from the abbey's central tower. When the priest puts on his vestments, he recites a specific prayer for each item; but the monk, too, says a prayer as he puts on his habit in the morning, so making it into a liturgical garment.

Naturally, most of these customs remain hidden from the outsider. The guest lives in the guesthouse, which is separated by heavy doors—always shut—from the *clausura*, the enclosure where the monks live. A monk is permitted to speak to an outsider only with the consent of the abbot. One does not get the impression that this regulation is particularly burdensome. In any case, the days are so full, with the times of prayer ("seven times"), the conventual Mass, the mealtimes, and the physical work that has to be fitted in, that deviation from the timetable is hardly practicable. The young monks almost always walk quite fast; they are purposeful and at the same time recollected. Approaching them, there is the impression, notwithstanding the smiling attention immediately given, that one has interrupted them. It seems as if the strictly regulated order of the day has opened the sluice-gates of a mighty current of thought that entirely fills the individual monk's attention.

"The loftiest aristocrat is not the feudal lord in his castle but the contemplative monk in his cell", writes the Colombian philosopher Gomez Davila. This kind of contemplative life is a solitary one, and the solitude is not diminished by the fact that it takes place in community, alongside so many other solitaries. At first glance it seems to have little to do with the notion of aristocracy, with concepts of higher and lower, that is, with the way people are related to the whole of society. However, after talking to one or another of the monks and reflecting on remarks that at the time seemed insignificant, incidental, and puzzling, I begin to see this solitude in an entirely different light: in this monastery, apparently, there are many monks who take quite literally Benedict's exhortation in the Rule that says that, when at prayer, they are in the presence of God and his angels. In a life lived in communal solitude, impregnated with the liturgy, it seems that the "cherubim and seraphim, thrones and dominations", the "heavenly hosts and angelic powers" referred to in the Preface of the Mass become tangible, even visible. Under the impression of a cosmic order of this kind, the concept of "aristocracy" would acquire an entirely new meaning.

If you ask the monks themselves about experiences of this sort, however, you will learn nothing more than what can be read in the words of the Psalmist, the Church Fathers, and the Gospel. This monastery is not the place for spiritual conferences, the sharing of theological experience, or the proclamation of manifestoes. Here, subjecting the liturgy, in its given-ness, to the pro-and-contra of debate would in all probability be regarded as inappropriate to the nature of the liturgy itself. For the outsider, no exposition of the principles underlying the monastery could be as instructive as simply observing its practice. Besides, anyone who has read the mystics will already have an intimation of the purposes and aims behind the cultivation of communal solitude.

Words cannot be a substitute for the impression made by one of the few spiritual exercises of the monk that are accessible to the visitor. This is the Mass that is celebrated by each priest-monk, alone, every morning after the Liturgy of the Hours. In late morning, of course, there is a lengthy conventual Mass with Gregorian chant, with priest, deacon, and subdeacon and the entire community; but according to an ancient rule each priest should celebrate one Mass every day himself, so the many priests of the community fulfill this obligation some hours before. Few of the monasteries of the Benedictine Order still observe this custom, and most of them have close links with Fontgombault.

The church is empty. It is still dark when the "private Masses" begin. This commonly used term is incorrect, of course, since, as one of the monks said, "the Mass is never something private." A small, plain stone altar stands in front of each pillar of the nave. One senses that there are more altars to each side of the choir, behind the choir grille. A long procession comes forth from the sacristy, one priest after another in colorful vestments, the white hood of his choir habit pulled down over his head, his hands holding a chalice covered with a cloth matching his vestments. Each priest is accompanied by a young altar server in a black habit. The procession divides, and one priest and his server halt at each of the little altars, until each of the twelve visible altars is occupied. Everywhere the same deep bow before the altar, everywhere the beating of the breast that accompanies the confession of sin, the synchronized approach to the altar step and the silent reading of the Introit psalm.

Sitting in the middle of the nave toward the back of the church, one sees a unique sight. We are accustomed to seeing the Mass take place at the focal point of a church building, but here it seems present everywhere, as in a hall of mirrors. The whole church perspective, concentrated on the choir, is alive with priests celebrating in solitude; each of them, with his solemn gestures, his uplifted hands, his bowing and genuflections, is conscious of doing something unique. Suddenly, from behind the high altar, the flash of a red vestment shows momentarily, at the raising of the Host. There is no wall, no chapel, no pillar at which the Sacrifice of the Mass is not being offered. Each priest's movements are slow; his lips show that he is reading word for word. For the span of this early morning Mass each celebrant has, as it were, stepped outside the monastery family—as Benedict, the ancient Roman patriarch, calls the Order he founded. The priestly office has created highly personal obligations, from which no community, no collective can dispense him. These quiet Masses, where the only noise is that made by the priests as they process in and out, indicate a possible effect of the liturgy—and they do this more convincingly than the musical and hieratic splendor of the great community liturgy: it is to be a chalice or receptacle for the ultimate substance of the person, a substance that evaporates when confronted by mere analysis.

There is just one moment in the day when the visitor can observe the order of movement disintegrate. The last communal prayer of the day is Compline, the evening prayer, which goes back to Benedict himself. At this point there are only two sources of light left in the nave: the sea of candles at the foot of the Mother of God of the Holy Death and the red dot of the sanctuary lamp that hangs before the tabernacle at the end of the choir. In their hymn the monks pray for protection against "phantasmata", demonic intrusions into their dreams; from their abbot they receive absolution from the sins of the day and, in the words of the Our Father, "Et dimitte nobis debita nostra, sicut et nos dimittimus debitoribus nostris", they are reconciled to one another. The abbot sprinkles each one of them with holy water, imparting a blessing to the whole monastery.

Now begins the time of silence that is not to be disturbed even by what might be considered a necessity. After three strokes of a bell the kneeling monks stand up and, for the first time, leave the choir in no particular order. Each monk finds a place somewhere in the church for private prayer. At the fringes of the candlelight one can discern individual dark shapes; but also, on the steps of the little altars, one suddenly comes across a more intense darkness that, by a slight movement, shows itself to be a human being.

A small dark heap is discernible before the gravestone of the first abbot, Petrus a Stella, and in the transepts, where one can hardly see one's hand in front of one's face, there are other such heaps that, in the twofold anonymity of the monastic habit and the darkness, seem not to be human at all. For a few seconds, when the monks dispersed in disorder at the end of Compline, there was a sense of something pulsating, as if each one were expectantly seeking a goal. After only a few steps, however, this goal is reached. The darkness removes all sense of space. If you sit still for a while, you feel that you are falling, peacefully and without suffering any violence.

Carl Schmitt wrote the following entry in his diary for August 1, 1948:

> It was not Robespierre who destroyed the monarch's crown, but Metternich. All that is left now is self-destruction, suicide. Restoration is a specific method of dealing with and destroying what is being restored. Why? Because it is self-destruction. So let us have no Restoration—whether of Church or State, of monarchy or of democracy, of throne or altar, of past forms of freedom or past forms of bondage and authority. *"We bring about order. It collapses. We restore the order and we ourselves collapse"* (Eighth Duino Elegy).

People are sometimes inclined to regard the life of the Fontgombault monks as an attempt at "restoration". This is understandable when one thinks of the influence the monastery has had. In its return to the sources of Benedictine life the abbey is not alone, nor has it been for some time now. Four other great monasteries have been founded from Fontgombault to respond to the increase in numbers. Closely allied with Fontgombault are the new foundations of the Monastery of Saint Madeleine du Barroux on Mont Ventoux (associated with a convent of nuns), the Monastery of Saint Joseph in Flavigny, Burgundy, the convent of nuns of Jouques, and a number of similar foundations and seminaries. These all exercise a great attraction and are growing steadily. This expansion of monastic life is unusual and unexpected in a time like ours, and it is important to understand that it is not connected with the idea of "restoration" associated with the name of Metternich; it is entirely lacking in political and social ambition. While the term "formation" creates a strong resonance in Fontgombault, it is never understood as the formation of particular groups, social classes, or elites, that is, as the formation of people outside the monastery.

Anyone who decides to become a monk in Fontgombault is concerned with the formation of a single human being: himself. Similarly, the fruits of this formation will be manifest to one person only, namely, the person thus formed. The Rule prescribes "stabilitas loci", by which Benedict means that the monk will spend his entire life in the same monastery; this precludes the kind of influence that can be exercised by traveling around. Anyone who wants to get to know the effect of this formation must himself set out on a journey to Fontgombault, deep in provincial France. What will he see there? First and foremost he will see the means employed in this formation, means that are inseparable from its ends; for this coincidence of means and ends, otherwise found only in art, is of the very essence of liturgy. Will this monastic movement, primarily issuing from France, ever have an influence on today's and tomorrow's Church? This is almost as improbable as the development that led from the call of Simon the fisherman and Matthew the tax collector to the universal Church.

6

Liturgy Is Art

In Germany, whenever there is a debate about the great Catholic liturgical tradition, it only needs someone to utter the accusation of "aestheticism", and it is all over. There is never any doubt which side has lost. To be charged with aestheticism is, for the most part, fatal for those trying to defend the liturgy. Even if we are Catholics, we come from a country under the dominance of a longstanding, militant Protestant culture, and the cultural imprint is at least as strong as the religious one. T. S. Eliot would go so far as to say that culture is the practical, concrete expression of religious faith; if that is true, the German Catholic is in a state of constant schizophrenia because his practical, cultural expression of faith is in conflict with his religion. The charge of aestheticism makes us feel guilty to the very marrow of our bones.

The German vice—philosophy—has firmly fixed the idea of a distinction between content and form in the minds of very diverse people. According to this doctrine, content and form can be separated from one another. What it regards as the authentic reality it calls the content: abstraction, the theoretical extract. By contrast, it regards bodies of flesh and blood, physical and tangible structures, as mere form, expendable and shadowy images. The idea is that those who occupy themselves with this external form remain at the peripheral level, the level of accidents, whereas those who go beyond the form reach the realm of eternal abstractions and so attain the light of truth. In this view, forms have become something arbitrary, sometimes even something worse—they are untrue; they are lies. Anyone who perceives the form and takes it seriously is in danger of being deceived. This is the trouble with the aesthete. He looks for truth in the wrong place, that is, in the realm of what can be seen, and he looks for it with the wrong (and forbidden!) means, that is, with his senses, taste, experience, and intellect. This philosophical rebellion against everything self-evident has given birth to the basic attitude of our generation, namely, an all-pervading distrust of every kind of beauty and perfection. Nowadays, the most withering condemnation is to say that something is "merely beautiful". Contemporary art favors things that are unfinished, fragmentary, broken. People actually despise the mastery of the craftsman's skills and rules—which are indispensable if one is to employ a complete language of forms. What is most irritating of all, for today's art lover, is when he is presented with nothing visible at all, just a few tentative strokes, cryptic traces, which are then taken up by our modern scribes and Pharisees in their interpretative excesses; the less there is to see, the more they have to say.

The crushing power of this contemporary attitude has inhibited Catholics and made them fearful and uncertain, faced with the task of defending their traditional form of prayer and sacrifice. This form, this mighty architecture composed of language, music, and gesture, was too visual, too full of concrete significance: it was bound to provoke the vehement opposition of our contemporaries. This form presented itself as something that demanded respect, that

knew nothing of its office of mere service; it did not consider that it could be exchanged for something else, that it
was subject to history. This form was so embodied and
three-dimensional that it prevented those who celebrated
it from being drawn to the movement that wanted to make
abstractions of the faith, to philosophize, historicize, and
sociologize it—as a so-called "new theology" suggested.
Furthermore, it possessed a dreadful, profoundly embarrassing and frivolous quality that, compared with the pal-
lor of the new message, was so inappropriate: it was
beautiful.

We cannot just laugh this off. It is difficult, if not impossible, to break out from one's time, and sometimes it seems
as if there is hardly anyone left unscathed, untouched by
this guilt feeling on account of liturgical beauty—a feeling
that seems to be demanded by the times in which we live.

I am making these preliminary points to demonstrate that
I know what I am doing as I work toward the topic of "liturgy and art". As always, when one has to exert oneself to
overcome some resistance, there is the danger of overshoot-
ing one's goal. I am well aware of this danger and am taking
the risk quite deliberately. What I am trying to do is not a
theological interpretation; I am pondering Christ and his deeds
from the vantage point of a particular life experience.

In his last work, a letter written in prison entitled "De
profundis", Oscar Wilde, the great provocateur, called Christ
an artist—the greatest artist. In all his provocative statements Wilde was always careful to tread on as many feet as
possible. Calling Christ an artist was bound to irritate the
pious; they were bound to suspect that he was trying to
drag Christ into his decadent artist's career. But the ratio-
nalists were equally annoyed; they thought they had finally
got rid of Christ and did not want to see him back in a

context as serious as that of art. I must admit that when I first read "De profundis" I found this "Christ the artist" a little far-fetched, particularly since Wilde did not try very hard to justify the idea. He listed Christ's simplicity, his way of looking at people, his imagination, his grace and poverty, as attributes of the artist. This is all well and good, but there is something disappointing about this lyrical and enthusiastic sermonizing, so untypical of Wilde. All the same, I could not shake off this equation of Christ and the artist.

My topic here is "liturgy and art". One might expect a disquisition on works of art that have been created for liturgical use; indeed, we shall come to that later. Initially, however, what interests me is the great work of art—and more than art—that the liturgy itself is. I want to contemplate the liturgy of the Latin Church from a single point of view, that is, as a work of art, so that we can get a better understanding of what it is by applying the criteria used for evaluating works of art. Now, the creator of a work of art is an artist; accordingly, I would point out that Christ is not only (as the Church teaches) the One who acts in every liturgy; he is also the One who, by his own deed, has equipped the liturgy, from its very first moments, with an artistic impulse. It is this artistic impulse that has wrought the development and shaping of the liturgy, from its core actions right up to the great living icon of a solemn pontifical Mass.

Jesus' whole life was marked by liturgical acts, whether in submitting to preexisting liturgical forms or in creating a new language of sacramental signs. From among all the events in Jesus' life I will take Holy Thursday as an example.

The Logos became flesh at a time we regard as Late Antiquity. Whether we wish to or not, we all draw nourishment, even today, from the inexhaustible treasure-house of this epoch in human history. Consciously or unconsciously we all take our standards, even today, from the works of the artists and writers of the ancient world. The most astounding artistic achievement of this period, however, has no single great originator: it was produced by a collective; the ancient peoples had the ability to translate natural objects into the language of art, creating a higher, second nature. It was born from the contemplation of nature, and at the same time it represented a new and ennobling creation. Who invented the Greek column? Who first transformed man, the creature who stands upright, into this form that is both abstract and, in its gently convex lines, organic? Who developed the Corinthian capital out of the leaves of the acanthus plant? Who made the Ionic capital with the curved horns of the sacrificial goats that were tied to a post in the place of sacrifice? In a similar way we find the most ancient use of timber building stylized and made into a decorative frieze in the marble temples of the great Classical period. Ancient peoples were given the grace to see the work of art contained in nature, and Christ possessed this gift of grace to the highest degree. Our faith tells us that he trod the earth "in the fullness of time", when this gift was in blossom.

The setting of Holy Thursday is well known. Christ assembles his disciples to celebrate the Jewish Paschal meal with them in Jerusalem. Thousands of pilgrims are in the city for the same purpose. This great flood of pilgrims has made it necessary to permit the celebration of the ritual meal over several days, not only on the feast day itself. We know, too, what Christ creates out of this festive meal, namely, the sacrificial and redemptive feast of the New Covenant, one of the greatest mysteries of a ministry that is replete with mysteries. How does he do this? One cannot imagine a greater distance between what he does, which is new, and the form that is to contain it, which is ancient. Christ will not interfere with ancient, sanctified customs that have come down from a time of earlier revelation. He speaks the old prayers and uses the old gestures. The one who drove the traders from the Temple—but not the priests—changes not a word when he founds the New Temple. He does not smash and dismember the ritual, although he, of all men, would have every right to do so. And afterward, *postquam coenatum est*, he takes a piece of the bread left over, and with this simple gesture, which disturbs nothing but seems to grow out of the rite like a new blossom, he imparts a new meaning to everything that preceded it and all that will follow.

At this point one might ask what is artistic about submitting to an old, traditional form. Artists, surely, are creators of something new; they are the ones who are constantly innovating with regard to form. Is not originality of form the hallmark of the artist? This, indeed, is how we think of things—we who live in a period of almost unimaginable collapse. Artists in the great productive periods never concerned themselves with the problem of originality. It was when they believed they were venerating and lovingly cultivating an inherited great form that they created something new, something unique, something that had never been seen before. What is new, really new—not some cobbled-together experiment—comes unconsciously when an individual breathes new life into what is old. So it is in art. Of course, in Christ's case we cannot speak of things of which he is "unconscious"; but we see with utter clarity how, with the highest degree of consciousness, he affirms the normative nature of this process. Then we come to his choice of the substance he will use for his act of instituting the Sacrament of the Altar. His choice is unexpected. When he utters the words "This is my body", should he not take a piece of the Paschal lamb from the table (considering his impending sacrificial death as the Lamb of God), rather than a piece of bread? No, because the bread that has become the Body of Christ fits in perfectly with what Jesus says, by way of preparation for Holy Thursday, about the grain of wheat; it also recalls the prayer in the Our Father concerning our daily bread and the warning that man does not live by bread alone but by every word that comes from God. Here, then, we have the bread that, at the same time, "was the Word of God".

The bread also announces the end of the blood sacrifice. The death of Jesus is to be the last bloody sacrifice. Is there not, however, something of the Greek artists' ability to transform and elevate nature in the way Jesus chooses to elevate a piece of bread to the level of the real sacrificial flesh of the God-man? At the same time, of course, there is a crucial difference between him and the Greek artist: the artist created his work "after nature", through contemplation and study, whereas Christ created the unbloody Sacrifice of the Mass in anticipation of his very real execution, with all its attendant horrors. We could say that, with his intuition and foreknowledge—for the meal of Holy Thursday is permeated with premonitions—he was painting a picture of his death, giving an artistic form to the pains of his execution, a form that perfectly and unmistakably manifested its profoundest core, that is, the love sacrifice that nourishes and redeems.

There is another event of Holy Thursday that deserves attention as a work of art. This is the washing of the feet, an action that can even form the basis for a theory of the nature of the work of art. Here, again, what takes place is not out of the ordinary, at least at first. Ablutions of this kind preceded a meal given to guests; they were part of religious and profane rites in the ancient world. What is extraordinary is the person washing. Christ washes his disciples' feet, to their utter confusion and amazement, since this service signifies subordination and obedience. Afterward he explains what he has done: "I have given you a sign." Might we be permitted to regard this explanation as less convincing than the sign itself? After all, the disciples had already heard him say several times that they should love and serve one another. I would like to risk the suggestion that, in view of the impending arrest of Jesus, this sign, this washing of the feet, was more than an effective illustration of a moral obligation. As with a work of art, we are in the presence of a reality that goes beyond what can be put into words. Something remains that cannot simply be understood: we must behold it, be astonished at it.

Art alone has the means of fulfilling Christ's command at the meal of Holy Thursday, namely, to make the *memoria*, the repeated, ever-new, making present of the sacrifice of Christ, to which he himself gave unbloody form. Great works of the world of art have this unlimited presence. A new passport photograph already looks as if it is being used by the police to identify an unknown corpse found in a river, whereas one of the mummy portraits from Fayum in Egypt, in spite of its two thousand years, gives us the vague feeling that we have just seen this man at the pizza restaurant. The hallmark of the work of art is its vitality, not its contemporaneity; something contemporary can be as dead as a doornail without being noticeable as such in its time. The historical document makes us feel the gulf that separates us from a past time; the work of art causes us to forget this gulf. Christ desired to make his sacrifice ever-present, and so he poured it into the shape of liturgical art.

Next, in the same spirit in which Christ gave a shape to his sacrifice, the Church began to create a frame for this greatest picture. Initially nothing was changed. In fact, the eyewitnesses of the Resurrection still went to the Temple—with hindsight, a completely illogical thing to do!—because Christ had set them the example of absolute reverence for inherited organic form. Once they no longer attended Temple worship, because they had been "thrown out of the synagogues", as Christ had predicted, they began to surround the sacrifice of Holy Thursday and Good Friday with the forms of synagogue worship. They prayed the ancient psalms as Christ had done, dying with a phrase from the psalms on his lips. In this process in the early Church, where liturgy is taking shape in the same way that new life develops, we are given an example of how *homo religiosus* carries out a reform of prayer (and this was of course the greatest of all reforms): he changes nothing; rather, he fills it with a new spirit. "In the fullness of time" the divine Master suspended a thread, as it were, in a saturated solution, and the crystals began to form. At an early stage, suddenly (as it seems to us) the liturgy was there in its complete and fully developed form.

Like the Magi, Judaism and paganism brought their treasures—kept safe for this moment—to the Church and constructed the bejeweled framework that was to surround the arena of mystery from now on. Christ had made it clear, right from the beginning, that his breaking of bread on Holy Thursday embodied the violent destruction of his body on Good Friday; and he had hinted that, nonetheless, there would be a meal in the future. So the disciples knew that, behind the veil of silence and absence covering the events in the Upper Room, other events, both past and future, were present, though hidden. There was the sacrifice of Abel, representing the prayer of the nations that had been given the original revelation; the sacrifice of Abraham, who had been given the promise; the sacrifice of Melchizedek, the mysterious figure who stands for the peoples who were not Jews. Then there is the future meal, which John had called "the Marriage of the Lamb". Very early on, the Church knew that the liturgy took place *in conspectu angelorum*; the angelic prayers of the *Gloria* and *Sanctus* do not invoke this presence: they affirm it. In fact the Eastern Church instructs the faithful to sing before the *Sanctus*: "Let us, who mystically represent the cherubim...."

The liturgy became a rich image with a welter of tiny details, greater than the sum of its parts; thus it must be contemplated and can never be entirely understood. Again it is artists who best spoke about the liturgy. I am thinking of the great Enguerrand Quarton in fifteenth-century France and his *Coronation of Mary* in Villeneuve-les-Avignon. Here God the Father and God the Son appear in the same form, faithful to Christ's word as reported in Saint John's Gospel: "He who sees me sees the Father." Both wear a red pluvial— priestly garments; the face of Mary, kneeling below them, is as white as a Host. She is the embodiment of the redemption, man newly created, which is the goal of the liturgy. The celebrating Trinity is surrounded by the orders of angels and archangels, thrones, powers, and dominations, martyrs, virgins, and confessors, all floating in a deep blue stratosphere above the earth. On the earth itself, however, we can see Moses before the burning bush and Gregory the Great celebrating the Mass during which the crucified Lord himself appeared on the altar at the Consecration. We see the tiny crosses of Golgotha, lost in the sea of history; we see the graves opening on the Last Day, and we glimpse the underworld, still waiting for redemption. Enguerrand Quarton's *Coronation of Mary* is a precise vision of the liturgy, making it clear that the Mass itself contains a vision, hidden beneath the veil of ancient words, beneath the silent gestures, beneath actions that are rooted in the earliest period of human history. The liturgy of the Mass is more than the proclamation of the teaching Christ. It is a great "Ecce homo": it exhibits and points to the silent Christ. It is infinitely more than the prayer of the faithful. It gives us a glimpse of something absolutely unthinkable: God at prayer.

The Council of Trent, in its teaching concerning the liturgy's sacred rites, said that these rites "contain nothing unnecessary or superfluous". This dictum, properly understood, again challenges us to regard the liturgy as a work of art. Influenced by the constant desecrations and the slide into neglect, we have again become accustomed to seeing the liturgy or particular aspects of it in terms of "validity". This is the language of Roman jurisprudence; it has its own tradition and justification, but basically it cannot help us when we come to ponder liturgical actions. The Mass is not a legal act, something that becomes "valid" in the presence of minimal requirements. Just imagine a canon lawyer trying to explain to a confused and hapless visitor at a modern Sunday celebration that what has taken place contained the various elements ("firstly, secondly, thirdly") and that therefore it was a "valid" Mass—he could even stamp a document for him, certifying that he had fulfilled his Sunday duty! No: the Mass is not some basic core activity to which various decorations can be added, according to opportunity, in order to heighten the participants' awareness. The rites "contain nothing unnecessary or superfluous". Who would dare to pretend to find "unnecessary or superfluous" things in a great fresco or a great poem? A masterpiece may contain gaps, less felicitous parts, repetitions, things that are unintelligible or contradictory—but never things that are unnecessary and superfluous. At all times there have been

people who made themselves ridiculous by trying to elim-
inate the "mistakes" in masterpieces, applying their half-
baked scholarship to Michelangelo's frescos and Shakespeare's
tragedies. Great works have a soul: we can feel it, alive and
radiant, even where its body has been damaged. The liturgy must be regarded with at least as much respect as a
profane masterpiece of this kind. Respect opens our eyes.
Often enough, even in the case of a profane work of art, if
we study conscientiously and ponder the detail, especially
the apparently superfluous detail, we find that the offend-
ing element comes unexpectedly to life; in the end it sometimes happens that we come to see it as a special quality of
the work. This is always the case with the rites of the sacred
liturgy. There is nothing in them that, given intensive contemplation, does not show itself to be absolutely saturated
with spiritual power. I would urge everyone to study and
ponder the meaning of any element of the rite—particularly
those parts that the reform of Pope Paul VI regarded as
"unnecessary and superfluous" (flying in the face of the warning given by the Council of Trent)—and they will find the
Council of Trent splendidly justified.

Here is an example. For a long time the many signs of
the cross made by the priest over the consecrated Host were
regarded as superfluous. Accordingly, because they were
superfluous, they were performed carelessly, as if the celebrant were flicking away a fly, and in the end they were
cut out. Even those who were attached to the old Mass did
not long lament their passing. Generally speaking, signs of
the cross are associated with the act of blessing, and nothing in the world could be more superfluous, it was thought,
than blessing a consecrated Host, since it already contained
every imaginable blessing! The interpretation of the function of these signs of the cross that I shall now suggest is

not authoritative from the point of view of liturgical scholarship, but I think it relevant and worth mentioning.

In fact these signs of the cross are not blessings. What are they then? I think the answer lies in their number. Twice the priest makes five signs of the cross, first three and then two. Let us begin with the two signs of the cross in the *Supplices te rogamus*, at the words "Corpus et sanguinem". These are not blessings, but references—and to what do they refer here? Nothing other than the fact that both substances, bread and wine, are of equal dignity since both together, and each separately, embody the whole Christ. Five is the number of Christ's wounds, and the five signs of the cross over the sacrificial gifts refer to the five wounds they (invisibly) bear, the wounds inflicted at the slaughter of the Lamb.

The three crosses refer to the Trinity and, in particular, to the fact that the Christ who bleeds from five wounds is one of the Persons of the Trinity. In these silent signs of the cross, therefore, we see in a nutshell a complete theology of Holy Mass and particularly of what takes place at the Consecration: the one Christ in two forms, the Son of God, lies with his wounds upon the altar of sacrifice; now the altar's narrow, long, linen cloths, on which the rubrics lay such stress, become really the grave cloths described in the Bible, found folded up in a corner of the sepulchre at the Resurrection. How could references to this event ever be "unnecessary and superfluous"?

Before concluding my reflections on the liturgy as a work of art, I would like to mention a number of short literary masterpieces it contains. I am referring to the orations—the Collects, Secrets, and Postcommunions—particularly those of Sunday. It seems that only secular philologists are in a position to see the literary and artistic value of these prayer formularies, which are certainly among the oldest constituent elements of the liturgical heritage:

> Most of the orations (priestly prayers) and prefaces are already found in the sacramentaries of the fifth through seventh centuries. From a specifically literary point of view, these texts already give us the substance of the Roman Missal. They are artifacts of high theological expressiveness, fashioned according to the canons of Late Latin art prose, of monumental simplicity and acute precision. They are so perfect that they have remained essentially unchanged, and today they still constitute the form of prayer of the Catholic Church.[1]

These orations originate in a linguistic world that is entirely different from the Latin of the Vulgate, which seems strangely primitive by comparison. In the orations we have the voice of the Roman Church, which adopted the heritage of the Roman Empire, transforming a universalism of state and culture into a spiritual universalism. Schooled by contact with the most brilliant examples of ancient rhetoric, the matter of the Church's prayer is here shaped, most elegantly, into priceless forms that are not unrelated to aphorism. Their expression is of a captivating graciousness. The Roman Church never showed herself more beautiful than in these orations, which are a school of sacramental sentiment. They express the distinctive nature of the Catholic Church, her concern for the sinner, her cautious guidance of souls, her dependence on the treasury of grace with which she has been endowed, her hope that hardened hearts will eventually be softened. And all this is put in such a polished way, communicating a joy in its own linguistic facility and lending a smile to these short sentences in spite of their serious

---

[1] *Kindlers Literaturlexikon*, vol. 4 (1968), col. 2721.

content. The orations remain at the level of classical generality, for they are the Church's public prayer for all people, and yet their substance is such that the individual silent reader can be deeply struck by them.

It is extremely hard to select one oration as an example, for the choice involves the renunciation of so many others of even greater beauty. Here then, at random, is the Secret from the Fourth Sunday after Pentecost: "Oblationibus nostris, quaesumus, Domine, placare susceptis: et ad te nostras etiam rebelles compelle propitius voluntates" (Be appeased, we beseech Thee, O Lord, by the offerings received from us, and graciously turn toward Thee even our rebel wills).

It is excruciatingly painful to descend from the heights of such a prayer to the kind of text that has been substituted for the old orations by the "liturgical reform"—a *coup de force* never seen before in history. I was once present at a Mass at which the lady entrusted with the General Intercessions uttered them in the nowadays customary amalgam of unctuous sentimentality and newspaper jargon; a friend whispered in my ear: "Lord, may our holiday photos turn out well!" Alas, satire's impotence shows itself particularly crass in such a case. In reality, the prayer for holiday photos has been surpassed ten thousandfold in the meantime. *Kitsch*—be it in language, music, painting, or architecture—has completely swamped the outward manifestation of the Church's public acts. The altars are covered with beige-colored Trevira, like we see on coffee tables; in one corner stand three fat candles in hand-thrown pot dishes, glazed with something that unpleasantly recalls bodily secretions, and the other corner of the table altar is adorned with a feature of roots and dried flowers, composed according to misunderstood principles of Japanese ikebana; in the center of the altar we see, not a cross, but the microphone. One wonders where the dish with the salted almonds is ... One thing is quite certain, to judge by the external appearance of these altars: they are not altars of sacrifice, nor are they intended to be.

These concrete halls, these carpeted floors, these massive pieces of birchwood furniture, the leather seats beside the altar, the wall-screen projector—all this so-solid style of interior architecture of a new or restored church is totally at odds with the idea that the sacred space, the sacred place is *terribilis*, terrifying, that it calls for reverence and must reflect this in the way it looks. Man's first religious act was to fence around the sacred place; in the old churches this was done not only by the walls that protected it against the outside world, but also by the inner arrangement: choir stalls, communion rails, grilles, choir screens and iconostases, all create a space for the Blessed Sacrament [*das Allerheiligste*, the Holy of Holies]. These things showed faith in God's bodily presence, a faith that was embodied in architecture.

If we want to assess the liturgy's vital power, there is no harm in looking at the way it is portrayed in secular art at any particular time. With this in mind I here reproduce a poem by Robert Gernhardt, which gives an idea of the way the new Church, that is, the Church after the Council, is seen. As can be imagined, Gernhardt has no connections with the Church; he is a brilliant nonsense-artist, satirist and humorist, but in the following poem the laughter seems to have evaporated—no doubt because his disgust was too strong. The subject of the poem is the church of the Assumption in Ahaus. It consists of a tower in the high Gothic style and a new concrete nave; but, one can safely assume, the author feels this particularly terrible example to be symptomatic. Ahaus is everywhere and has been for a long time. The mentality that produces such buildings is still dominant.

Saint Horten in Ahaus

There stands a church in Ahaus
Saint Horten's is what they call it,
and even living near this place
will shrivel up your spirit.

The thing towers up and sits there
stupid in concrete.

The old church in Ahaus
was torn down; the new replaced it.
Only the tower was left there.
You can keep the rest; it's just shit.

Gray and bare
it oppresses the air,
stupid and brutal.

The Ahaus church—you don't know
whether to laugh or cry.
It's sad what they get up to,
hilarious
to the stranger's eye.

They're even proud of the crap,
stupid and complex.

Saint Horten's church in Ahaus
in another thousand years
will tell those who have lost all heart
about our pride and sneers:

tormented by choice,
stupid totally.

Just think what significance the Catholic liturgy had for the work of James Joyce. Joyce had no sympathy at all for the Church, and many Catholics may find his novel *Ulysses*, one of the greatest works of modern literature, almost unbearably malicious. In it, however, if there is a tangible aesthetic structure, a final cultural authority, it is the old Latin Mass, which, with its ritual and language, provides a kind of anchor to Joyce's rank linguistic extravagance. *Ulysses* begins with the psalm "Judica", recited at the altar step in the old Mass.

Traces of the liturgy are everywhere in this book, but there is a particularly memorable scene in which the novel's Jewish hero, Leopold Bloom, mocking and aloof, attends a Mass; he cannot suppress a certain respect, against his will, for what he sees there. Joyce could never have imagined that he was describing a form of worship that was in mortal danger; for him the Mass was something unchangeable and objective, an institution that had become second nature: he could attack it because, secretly, he knew it was indestructible. *Ulysses* could never have been written without the old liturgy; here we sense the liturgy's immense cultural and creative power. Even its opponents could not avoid being in its shadow; they actually depended for nourishment on its aesthetic substance.

The liturgy of the reform and its adornments will never be able to constitute a seminal fact in the life of the nations. It is too anemic, too artificial, too little religious, too lacking in form to do this. The old liturgy, on the other hand, is not as poorly equipped for the terrible trials it has to face as we might often think, beholding its daily woes. The struggle against the old liturgy has helped us toward greater insights into its nature. Initially it must have felt like a deathblow when the liturgy was driven from the magnificent old churches that had been created for it. Then, however, it became clear that it was the churches that died, once the spirit of the sacred vanished from them; the liturgy itself stayed alive, albeit in lamentable circumstances. For it is the liturgy that produces all that is solemn and festive—art can contribute nothing essential to it. Once, I recall, the dean of a cathedral, very annoyed, asked me why on earth I wanted to go to the old Mass; after all, he said, very elaborate orchestral Masses were celebrated in the cathedral from time to time. I simply could not make him see that a low Mass in the old rite, read silently in a garage, is more solemn than the biggest church concert with spiritual trimmings. We have come to see, in a time without holy images, without sacred places and sacred music, that the old liturgy was itself the greatest possible image; we have realized that, if there is ever to be significant religious art again, this art will come from liturgy that expresses the sacred.

The period of iconoclasm in Byzantium lasted for more than a hundred years; it, too, contained a certain tincture of ecumenical calculation—Islam, of course, was hostile to images. In the nineteenth century Dom Prosper Guéranger had already predicted the Roman iconoclasm that was to proliferate in the wake of the Second Vatican Council: he called it the "antiliturgical heresy". In Byzantium, after vast destruction, the holy images were victorious. Resolute monks had taken some of the icons and hidden them. We, too, need many resolute priests who will guard and keep for us the sacred rite of the Incarnation.

7

Kneeling, Standing, and Walking

A Correct Understanding of "Active Participation"

I

Prior to the liturgical reform, Catholics were known by the fact that they knelt to pray; it was something that made an impression on outsiders. Since that time, however, the kneelers have been removed from many churches, and new churches are often built without any kneelers at all. Communion rails, where people used to kneel to receive Holy Communion, have generally disappeared altogether. Kneeling is now supposed to be a sign of private devotion; one hears it said that the early Church always stood for the liturgy. Standing is supposed to be a sign of the Resurrection and, hence, the only appropriate attitude for those performing Christian worship.

The debate about correct posture during the liturgy is particularly difficult because arguments from Church history and archaeology are almost always used for political and tactical reasons. Nowadays, in many cases, the people who say that the congregation should stand to pray are those who want to do away with adoration of the eucharistic Christ. It may be true that, in ancient times, standing to pray expressed reverence and solemnity and that the worshipper, in standing, had a sense of being destined for resurrection and of proclaiming the resurrected Christ; this may be interesting information, but it does not produce the same consciousness in us. For us, standing has lost all significance as a specific gesture.

When I was young, Catholics and Protestants used to come together for religious family occasions, as still happens in most German families. When Mass was read, the Catholic aunts knelt for the Consecration, while the Protestant uncles remained standing. What this said to me was, "We respect your devotion, but it is has nothing to do with us." Here, standing was decidedly at odds with solemnity and devotion; it had a purely civil quality, something to do with "good manners". It was felt to be something painfully awkward. Now, however, the mature Christian knows that there is nothing specifically religious about "good manners", and so the embarrassing standing was replaced by the more comfortable sitting.

Sitting is a genuine invention on the part of the liturgical innovators: no one sat in the ancient Church. If you enter a Roman basilica or a Byzantine church you will see immediately that there are no seats or pews in them (except where, in Rome, they have been introduced subsequently). Even the floors, often richly encrusted with precious stones, show that they were not made to be covered up by chairs. In the Byzantine Church those who are frail can lean on small frames arranged by the wall; in the Coptic Church some people are provided with T-shaped sticks to put under their arms, but apart from these aids people stand through the entire ceremony, which lasts for several hours. Standing is interrupted only by the many deep bows they make, touching a hand to the ground, and the *proskynesis*, in which they kneel down and touch their foreheads to the ground.

Kneeling in the Christian liturgy has two roots, which can be traced back to a single root. The first is the New Testament, where we read: "And he fell down and worshipped him." This expression is not restricted to Saint John's account of the healing of the blind man: it occurs again and again whenever someone suddenly realizes the divinity of Jesus. This New Testament kneeling is utterly unliturgical: it occurs when someone is momentarily overwhelmed; it is the response to a gracious epiphany. In the New Testament one has the impression that the person is thrown to his knees by a lightning flash of insight. At this moment, on his knees, he sees more than those standing around him, and he can find no better word in response to what he sees than the word *Credo*. How does this involuntary, utterly personal kneeling—the work of a moment—find its way into the framework of a suprapersonal and supratemporal liturgy?

Although the essential elements of the liturgy can be found in the earliest testimonies of the apostolic period, the liturgy's internal architecture could only unfold when an external architecture had been created for it. For the first three centuries the liturgy was celebrated, not in buildings specially made for it, but in the famous Catacombs and in private houses and provisional locations—expressing the vicissitudes of the early Church's life. It was Emperor Constantine the Great who erected the first churches, immediately after his victory over Maxentius in A.D. 313, namely, the Lateran Basilica, Old Saint Peter's, and Saint Paul's Outside the Walls, the Church of the Holy Sepulchre in Jerusalem, and the predecessor of today's Hagia Sophia in Constantinople. "The great imperial architecture comes at the very beginning of Christian church-building" [1]—this insight from

---

[1] Gerke, *Spätantike und frühes Christentum* (Baden-Baden, 1967).

the world of art history is particularly significant for a liturgy that is most intimately fused with ecclesiastical architecture.

Examining early Christian representations of the Madonna and the saints—in a tradition that extends into the Middle Ages—one often notices the curtains that are either pushed to one side or else form a decorative envelope for the figure portrayed. These curtains come from Byzantine court ceremonial as practiced by Constantine. Even this emperor's predecessors no longer followed the model of the Augustan (and ultimately republican) prince but had adopted the style of government and self-awareness of the great oriental kings. The *princeps* had become the *basileus*.

The most important of the ceremonies with which the emperor surrounded himself was the imperial "epiphany"—in which the emperor was manifested to his court in all his glory. The emperor and his family, dressed in bejeweled finery, assembled behind a curtain, while the court waited expectantly in the palace hall. When the curtain was opened, revealing the emperor, the court sank to their knees in *proskynesis*.

There is clearly a strong association between a scene such as this and the view of the opened tabernacle, its veil drawn to one side, the ciborium displayed, its veil removed, and the congregation on their knees before it in prayerful adoration. Here we have the germ from which the liturgy's gesture of kneeling adoration developed.

Confronted with this explanation of the origin of kneeling at Mass—the cult of the emperor in late antiquity—the enlightened democrat, of course, will be confirmed even more in his rejection of kneeling. Indeed, one could argue about this if this adoption of the epiphany ceremonial had resulted in a pompous and overblown liturgy, alienated from its true nature. The precise reverse is the case, however:

Constantine and the bishops of his time added this epiphany ceremony to the liturgy because they knew that the entire liturgy is the epiphany of Christ. The early Church celebrated the liturgy behind strictly closed doors; the secret location, the danger involved in assembling together, and the initiation of the participants—all these things represented the veil concealing Christ, until the eucharistic moment of his manifestation had arrived. Once the Church, in her basilicas, had stepped forward into public view, the liturgy had to find clearer signs to bring the mystery to the believers, and to do so gradually, until all its fullness was displayed: from the epiphany of the divine Word to the unveiling of the sacred vessels and, finally, to the bodily Presence. The man who follows this unfolding event with devotion and lives his life in anticipation of the moment of Christ's manifestation will be able, if he is very fortunate, to fall to his knees, overwhelmed by the insight of faith, like one of the New Testament figures.

Kneeling to pray where there are no kneelers, as in the very old churches or the all-too-new ones, one may be in an even better position to realize what one is doing. There are beautiful old pews in some of the churches, but it must be admitted that such devotional furniture can suggest an inappropriate atmosphere of settled comfort. Here, on the helpfully slanting, upholstered prie-dieus, kneeling—which should be a highly significant act—almost becomes just another kind of sitting. And if a church has no kneelers, that does not mean that one should not kneel. When the blind man fell down at Jesus' feet, there was no prie-dieu to hand. This is not to excuse the removal of the kneelers, which was done for a specific purpose (to create a new mentality), but their absence could prompt us to instill a new spontaneity into our kneeling before the incarnate Word.

When should one kneel at Mass? From the foregoing remarks it is quite clear: genuflection and kneeling signal and accompany the moments of the divine epiphany within the liturgy. The believer kneels down when entering the sacred space, the church, like Moses, who heard a voice from the burning bush telling him to take off his shoes because he was standing on holy ground. We genuflect during the *Credo* and in the Last Gospel (the Prologue of Saint John's Gospel), recalling the Incarnation in which God becomes visible. After uttering the words of Consecration, the priest venerates the sacred sacrificial gifts by genuflecting, and the people are kneeling. The congregation is kneeling as the priest shows them the Lord's Body, and Communion is received kneeling. Finally the faithful receive the priest's blessing on their knees, expressing the fact that it is a blessing from heaven, "from above".

These are the events of the liturgy that are associated with kneeling. They are all special moments of divine presence. All other parts of the liturgy are celebrated standing: the entry of the priest, the prayer before the altar, the *Kyrie*, *Gloria*, the Collect. The people sit for the reading. They stand for the Alleluia, the Gospel, the Creed, the Offertory, the Preface, the *Sanctus*; then, after the Canon, they stand for the *Pater noster* and *Agnus Dei*. After receiving Communion, they stand for the Postcommunion and, after the priest's blessing, the Last Gospel. Those who want to join, step by step, in the celebration of Holy Mass as a sacred drama, expressing the various parts in the appropriate body language, should respect this order of things. It has been forgotten, like many other liturgical rules. The customs of popular piety have obscured the special meaning of kneeling—veneration of the divine epiphany—by obliterating the distinction between standing and kneeling: the people kneel during many other parts of the liturgy as well. It became customary to kneel for the entire course of Low Mass. In many places (and of course I am speaking throughout of the celebration of Mass according to the classic Roman Rite) the congregation kneels even during the priest's *Confiteor* and during the Offertory. This is liturgically "incorrect". If we are seeking to instill a new spiritual dimension into the old order of liturgical prayer, it is perhaps worth recalling the special meaning and expressiveness of kneeling and its actual liturgical function.

In case there may be any misunderstanding of my remarks on the appropriate posture to be adopted during the various prayers of the Mass, I hasten to say that in Catholic Church tradition the congregation's oft-quoted "active participation" in the celebration of Mass is by no means interpreted as narrowly as is now usual. The believer can "participate actively" in a variety of ways. He can follow the priest step by step along the high road of the mysteries, subordinating his prayers, as the priest does, to the traditional gestures—standing, bowing, moving to one side or the other, and so on. But he can also simply contemplate the work of Christ that is carried out in Holy Mass; in doing this he does not necessarily have to join in every one of the liturgy's prayers, but may silently and in solitude adore the miracle that is taking place before his eyes. It is one of the greatest paradoxes of Holy Mass that, with all its liturgical strictness, it particularly facilitates prayer that is radically personal and contemplative. Yes, it is "incorrect" to remain kneeling for the whole course of Mass, or during the *Gloria* or the Offertory, but no one should be prevented from doing so. This "private" kneeling does not mean that the individual has abandoned the community and its fellowship (to which the liturgy actually invites us); this is one of the abundant wellsprings that show the spiritual superiority of the classical rite.

II

What I have said about kneeling during the liturgy shows that, by kneeling, the participants are venerating the epiphany of Jesus Christ, that is, all those moments in which his bodily presence is recalled or which are filled with this same bodily presence. In all the other parts of the Mass, according to the most ancient custom, the congregation stands. This act of standing, prescribed explicitly for a whole series of prayers (*Gloria*, *Credo*, *Pater noster*, but also for the *Angelus*, the *Magnificat*, and the antiphons of our Lady), is hard for us to appreciate as a religious act nowadays. Standing, as a form, a conscious act, is something that occurs all too rarely in our lives, and the liturgical forms of reverence draw their vitality from their origin, just as the sacred substances of bread and wine do from their intimate contact with everyday life: the sacraments are acts of Incarnation, that is, ever-new ways in which the Creator enters the world he has created. The lack of form in our world has destroyed the countless links between liturgy and everyday life—or at least it has rendered them harder to see.

The most formless way of assembling together is the buffet reception, which is taken standing. From a distance it looks like a group of people who have been waiting for the bus so long they have started talking to one another. There is nothing festive about it. At concerts given by famous musicians, it is still possible to experience "standing ovations"—where everyone stands as the master returns to the stage. Usually, however, people stand only because there are not enough seats. No argument from archaeology can gainsay it: standing, proved to have been the central attitude of worship in early Christianity, has lost its meaning as far as we are concerned, or at least that meaning is far from obvious to us. Furthermore, as we get older, protracted standing can be painful and hinder our prayer. The meditative sitting practiced in Asiatic religions seems to be more helpful in this regard.

To develop convincing images of what is meant by sacred standing one needs to look back to the early period of Christian art. For Christians, however, looking back is never a matter of poking around in dusty old chests: it is as if we are entombed in a dark cave—time—and are looking toward the radiant sunlight at the end of a long tunnel. In the golden mosaic cupolas of Byzantine churches, the Pantokrator, the enthroned Christ, is surrounded by the standing figures of angels and saints. They stand around Christ as his guard and retinue. He returns, to be met by the host of the redeemed, carrying weapons (as do many angels) or books that put into language the mystery that is taking place. If prayer is understood in a restricted sense as speaking to God, these figures are not praying. At this specific moment they cannot pray, because the distinction between them and God has been transcended; these figures who stand in the presence of God have been transmuted, translated to God's side; they have become God's organs, celebrating, extolling, and proclaiming his appearing; they shine like the planets that receive their light from the sun.

The next image is not an artistic creation but a historical tableau: the women and the Apostle John stand beneath the Cross. No doubt they prayed as they stood there, but at this unique moment, at the watershed of world history, there was something more important to them than prayer: eyes and ears were fixed on the Crucified; they did not want to lose a single movement of their dying Lord. This is how Jesus' dying words have come down to us. Their act of standing beneath the Cross was more than a mere waiting; standing there, they made up the time the disciples in Gethsemane lost by sleeping. To "assist" means both to be present and to help. Now, of course, it was too late for help. But there was something not entirely passive about the eyewitnesses' watching and waiting. The attitude of those standing beneath the Cross shows that they were united with Jesus as he underwent his life's last moments; they wanted to die with him. They too had been translated to God's side.

We can go even farther back as we plumb the depth of meaning of the act of standing. There is the image of the sons of Israel, prior to their Exodus from Egypt, eating that strange nocturnal meal of freshly killed lambs and bitter herbs, after they had daubed the fresh blood on the doorposts of their houses. There is something unnerving about these people standing around the tables, "their loins girt", ready for the march, taking their sacrificial meal in silence while, outside, the angel of death was killing the Egyptians' firstborn. This standing was not actually prayer, either; it was associated with the busy activity of dismembering the animal. Those standing were fulfilling a divine command that bade them be unreservedly ready. While a dire fate, decreed by God, befell the Egyptians, the elect stood ready, as soon as the sign was given, to carry out God's work in the way he had specified. However alien this Exodus meal, with its context of sacrifice and vengeance, may be to us; or rather, however remote from us it has become as a result of Christ's teaching, it was so significant that the early Christians, and Jesus himself, saw the Last Supper in connection with it. Now Jesus was the slaughtered Lamb, and so the meal was eaten standing. It was not that the Last Supper, when Jesus and the disciples reclined at table, was simply appended to it; rather, the early Christians did justice to the sacrificial character of this meal by linking it with the rites of the Exodus.

All these various modes of standing, and the dispositions of mind and heart associated with them, are what is meant when people say that the Christian celebrates the risen Christ by standing to pray. It is easier, of course, to arrange one's bodily posture than one's state of mind. In our age we are faced with the veritable inversion of signs and their meanings. Whereas the early Christians, by standing at the liturgy, expressed the fact that they were celebrating a sacrificial meal, it often happens that contemporary worshippers stand to express the opposite—that they are *not* participating in a sacrifice. Kneeling speaks an unmistakable language; standing does not. Nowadays standing is felt to show less reverence than kneeling. This is something that comes to us from secular history and its upheavals. It also has something to do with the massive pews that are customary in Germany: a person standing in one of these pews looks rather like a schoolboy or schoolgirl who has been summoned by the teacher to answer a question. Pews are basically Protestant: they are designed to facilitate the hearing of long sermons. When new churches are being built, people should perhaps learn from the example of the Romance countries with their lightly built straw-seated chairs, which can be turned into a kneeler at a stroke. It will probably take a great effort to reacquire a grasp of what is meant by genuinely liturgical standing; churches will need to be built to facilitate this posture, and the faithful will need to have in their hearts the image of the angels and saints standing around their Lord.

III

"Procedamus in pace!"

Like standing and kneeling, walking also has a specific liturgical meaning. There is an ancient connection between walking and praying. Even the Jews of the Old Testament remembered their forty years' desert wandering, in which they carried with them the Ark of the Covenant, as a great penitential march of preparation. When the Ark was brought into the Temple at Jerusalem, it was carried in procession, at the head of which came King David, dancing. Jews of the period after the exile in Babylon, making their pilgrimage from distant lands to Mount Zion, saw their ascent to the holy mountain as a procession of prayer, as many of the psalms bear witness. We can also think of the great pagan processions, the Panathenaea, which also led up a sacred mountain, accompanying the image of the goddess. The soul's movement toward God can be expressed with special clarity in the metaphor of walking; to the devoted person it can even become visible: what would otherwise remain merely an act of the mind or an emotional state becomes something objective, so to speak, as we walk.

In the Roman liturgy the procession originally had the same significance as in the Greek, but the tendency in the Western liturgy, with its increasing emphasis on reason and the intellect, was to restrict this element. For the early Christians each Mass began with a procession. The pagan and Jewish models of processions were filled with new meaning under the influence of the two great processions of the New Testament, namely, Christ's entry into Jerusalem on Palm Sunday and the Via Dolorosa on Good Friday. Each procession, the glorious and the painful, has Christ at its center; people accompany Christ and in doing so profess their faith in his divine-human presence. As can still be seen in the Missal, the community of Rome used to assemble at a particular church prior to each Mass and proceeded thence to the church where the liturgy was to take place. In the French Benedictine monasteries that have remained faithful to the old rite, each Sunday and holy day Mass begins with a procession of this kind through the cloister. There are special hymns for these processions; they can be found in the *Processionale* that is published by the Abbey of Solesmes. Yet again we see that the reformers of the Mass, preoccupied with their notion of early Christianity, were intent only on impoverishing and curtailing; they were actually pursuing a late Catholic Puritanism rather than drawing on the wealth of forms of worship of the first millennium.

Those who cherish Catholic tradition should devote some attention to this *Processionale*. In many places there would not be enough room for a procession at the beginning of Mass, but there are places where it might be possible. Walking slowly in procession to the accompaniment of Gregorian hymns opens up a whole new world of spirituality. Gregorian hymns are not written in march tempo; prayer must always be a highly personal act if it is to have any meaning, and Gregorian chant has a power that does not compel; it actually prevents people walking in step and having identical thoughts.

Christ is present in this procession in the person of the priest, surrounded by incense and candles, which are his liturgical emblems, so to speak (analogous to the national emblems displayed in the presence of a high state official). In the person of the priest, Christ enters Jerusalem—represented by the particular church building—to consummate the sacrifice of Golgotha. As he enters the church he is greeted by the Introit psalm, which is nothing other than a processional chant; it should accompany the priest's entrance, although it is not until after the prayer at the altar step that the priest quietly prays its verses.

The next procession at Mass is the Gospel procession. It is accompanied by the processional chants of the Gradual and Alleluia. This procession can be still seen at High Mass, when the deacon goes to read the Gospel. But even when the priest alone reads Low Mass, the removal of the Missal from the Epistle side to the Gospel side must be seen as a procession, accompanied by candles and incense. For the reading of the Gospel is far more than "proclamation": it is one of the ways in which Christ becomes present. The Church has always understood it to be a blessing, a sacramental, effecting the remission of sins, as is affirmed by the "Per evangelica dicta deleantur nostra delicta" that recalls the *Misereatur* after the *Confiteor*. The Gospel's sacramental character, effectively remitting sins, is surely the decisive argument for its being read in the sacred language. The liturgical signs of the procession make this character particularly clear.

As for the Offertory procession in the classical rite, unfortunately only traces of it are left. Sadly, this has resulted in the Offertory's significance being more and more obscured. If we want to understand what the Offertory really is, we must look to the Byzantine Church. There the deacon bears the veiled gifts through the church, surrounded by incense and candles, while the faithful bow profoundly or even fall to the ground. The unveiling of the gifts is venerated as the terrible moment when Christ was stripped of his clothes. The Eastern Church sees the whole liturgy—with its high point at the Consecration—as an uninterrupted sequence of instances in which Christ becomes present. The Western argument is that it is not appropriate to venerate the bread, which, though destined for consecration, is not yet consecrated; to the Orthodox this seems equivalent to saying that Christ is not worthy of veneration until he has been sacrificed. However, even in the Roman liturgy the subdeacon brings the gifts, veiled, to the altar, even if he takes the shortest route (from the credence table to the altar) and is not accompanied by candles and incense. The Offertory psalm indicates that at one time a procession used to take place at this point. In many churches it may be possible to place the credence table at such a distance from the altar that the subdeacon's journey between the two can once again suggest a procession. When new churches are being built, those responsible should be careful not to fill the spaces with too much furniture; room should be left for processions.

The final procession at Mass, apart from the priest's departure (which coincides with the moment of the final blessing, or of the many blessings, imparted as he leaves), is the Communion procession. Rarely, one suspects, is it experienced as such. The Communion psalm is meant to accompany the faithful as they go to receive the Host—Christ present—flanked by candles. The Tridentine rubrics order the priest to say the Communion psalm after Communion and the ablution of the chalice, but it is no infringement of the spirit of these rubrics if the schola sings the Communion psalm, as envisaged, during the Communion of the faithful; in this way the latters' slow progress to reception of the Eucharist acquires the dignity of a great prayer.

If the liturgy is seen as a sequence of processions, Pius X's often misunderstood reference to the "active participation" of the faithful in the liturgy suddenly becomes easy to grasp. One can hardly imagine any greater participation than walking behind Christ and going to meet him. Walking along in a procession, it all seems quite simple.

8

Station: Before Entering the Cathedral

To modern man the genealogy of Jesus as found in the first sixteen verses of Saint Matthew's Gospel is, at best, an absurd concatenation of sounds. The succession of Old Testament names, in quasi-Greek or Latin versions, recalls an incantation or spell; it is both grotesque and comical. It is as if a multitude of dwarfs, with strange Van Dyke beards and pointed caps, is joined together by their generative organs to form a human edifice, an artistic tower of humanity. We find these venerable patriarchs, each one standing on another's head, sculpted into the pointed arch of the entrance porches of Gothic cathedrals. On the walls we see Jesse, wearing slit Turkish trousers, sleeping on a grassy hillock, while from his loins a creeper issues, tree-high, its twisted foliage revealing the faces of tiny, anxious old men looking out; they are all connected to each other, and ribbon-like labels announce their strange names. David and Solomon, Jacob and Joseph are the only familiar characters among others such as Perez and Amminadab, Rehoboam and Asa, Jehoshaphat and Jotham, Hezekiah, Jechoniah, Shealtiel and Zerubbabel.

The genealogy of Jesus is the Gospel for the Feast of the Nativity of Mary on September 8; it is also read on August 16, the Feast of Saint Joachim, Mary's father, who is not mentioned in the genealogy at all. It can be seasonally hot on both feasts. Then the deacon sings this genealogy, dressed in his gold-embroidered dalmatic and surrounded by servers carrying candles and thuribles, perspiring profusely into the white linen cloth that encloses his neck. "Abraham autem genuit Isaac, Isaac autem genuit Jacob, Jacob autem genuit Judam et fratres eius. . . ." So it goes on: fourteen generations from Abraham to David, another fourteen generations from David to the captivity in Babylon, and finally another fourteen generations, from Babylon to the birth of Jesus Christ.

Is this really a piece of the Christian message? Is this genealogy with its three groups of fourteen—clearly stylized—something more than an archaic ritual? Jesus' family tree (abbreviated by three kings in order to preserve the rhythm of the three fourteens) is here presented by Matthew in such a way that it emphatically repeats the name of David: fourteen represents the numerical value of the three Hebrew consonants that frame the name David. Jesus Christ is the "son of David"; the family tree is meant to prove this. He is the one about whom Isaiah uttered this strange warning: "Hear then, O house of David! Is it too little for you to weary men, that you weary my God also? Therefore the Lord himself will give you a sign. Behold, a virgin shall conceive and bear a son, and shall call his name Immanuel."

For thousands of years it was accepted that descent, pedigree, gives evidence of election, of legitimacy, substantiating the claim to lordship; all juridical relationships, public and private, were seen in the context of descent. This is something the Western nations and those marked by them have utterly forgotten. The solemnity that once—even at the beginning of our century—surrounded the "family of royal blood" is now reapplied to the "elected parliament"

or the "elected president". Yet David's family tree continued to be traced up to the recent past. Emperor Haile Selassie
of Ethiopia bore the title "King of Zion" and "Lion of
Judah"; for three thousand years a rumor went around in
his family that it owed its origin to King Solomon and the
Queen of Sheba—much as a certain Prince Massimo proudly
told Napoleon that he was descended from Quintus Fabius
Maximus Cunctator. Up until the fall of Emperor Haile
Selassie in 1974, his genealogy used to be sung by the ecclesiastical singers; it was divided into sections, each containing seven generations, and all the children of the Ethiopian
"House of David" used to learn the last seven generations
of their family tree by heart, so that they could recite them
on solemn occasions. Just as we find in Matthew, only the
fathers and sons were named; and, as in Matthew, female
names cropped up in the long series from time to time,
when something important was associated with these particular mothers.

The unsuspecting reader is quite taken aback when he
comes to the end of Jesus' genealogy. Its purpose is to demonstrate Jesus' descent from King David in a factual way
and using symbolic numbers. Thirty-nine times we read
"genuit" (begat), since the genealogy's author is not afraid
of seeming monotonous when it is a case of accuracy. Suddenly, however, when he has to draw his conclusion from
this long series of generations, he omits the word "begat":
"Jacob begat Joseph, the husband of Mary", and he continues, "of whom Jesus was born, who is called Christ".
According to Matthew, therefore, Joseph did not beget Jesus.
A great genealogy has been laid before us—to show that it
does not show Jesus' descent. Does this mean that Emperor
Haile Selassie had more claim to be a "son of David" than
Jesus?

The early Christians openly recognized the difficulty presented by this passage of Scripture. Saint Justin, as early as the second century, asserted that Mary also came from the house of David. The *Protoevangelium of Saint James*, also a very early text, confirms Mary's descent, and the entire Christian tradition adopted this view. Christian art, too, often sees Mary as a "daughter of David". In many depictions of the Jesse Tree, Mary comes at the end of the sequence of generations, and the problematical Joseph has entirely disappeared. The Church has never simply rejected traditions that cannot be substantiated. She has always left much in place, aware that, ultimately, the canonical Gospels are themselves fruits of tradition. According to the Jewish custom, it is said, it was preferable to marry one's close relatives. Mary may have been Joseph's cousin. This makes sense of the puzzling conclusion of Jesus' genealogy. Then we read again Matthew 1:16—"Joseph the husband of Mary, of whom Jesus was born"—and a doubt arises at this point: Is not the explanation given by tradition simply too perfect, too smooth, too reassuring?

In a family tree that traces only the male line, every deviation from this rule must be very significant. This is particularly the case where, as in Jesus' genealogy, it seems to lead to Mary, yet it is not entirely convincing in fitting her in. However, the other women in Jesus' genealogy are also puzzling. Why are they important enough to break the patriarchal principle? Pious exegetes find them embarrassing. Not all of these women were exemplary characters, either; but all of them were highly peculiar.

First we come to Tamar, the Canaanite woman. She becomes the daughter-in-law of Judah, one of the twelve sons of the patriarch Jacob. Before she becomes pregnant, Yahweh kills her husband, who "was evil in the sight of the Lord". The Book of Deuteronomy provides the "levi-rate" solution to such a childless widowhood: a brother of the dead man must marry the widow; if he produces a son with her, this child is regarded as the dead man's descen-dant and heir, so that "his name may not be blotted out from Israel." In Tamar's case, her brother-in-law was called Onan. At his father's command he married Tamar. "But Onan knew that the offspring would not be his; so when he went in to his brother's wife he spilled the semen on the ground, lest he should give offspring to his brother." God punishes this act with death, and Tamar is a widow again. Judah's last son, Shelah, is still too young for the levirate duty, but the father seems also to have feared that a curse rested on every marriage with Tamar, and he tried to find a way of avoiding this third marriage. Then Tamar put off her widow's garments, dressed herself as a prostitute and stood by the roadside, evidently sure that Judah would never miss such an opportunity. And indeed, by this stratagem, she gets twins from her father-in-law. Judah has to admit, "She is more righteous than I, inasmuch as I did not give her to my son Shelah."

However, Tamar, with her son Perez whom she had with her father-in-law, became an ancestor of King David. Six generations later we come across Rahab, not a merely appar-ent prostitute, but a real one, of the town of Jericho. Her entry into the House of David is described in the Book of Jonah. Joshua sends two spies into the enemy town of Jer-icho. The two men hide under bundles of flax on the roof of Rahab's house, which is by the city wall. Rahab is con-vinced of Yahweh's almighty power: "The Lord your God is he who is God in heaven above and on earth beneath." She lets the spies down the city wall in a basket and shows them their escape route. In return the spies swear to her that she and her entire family will be spared when Jericho is stormed; a scarlet cord will identify her house.

When, finally, the walls of Jericho collapse at the sound of the trumpets and the shouting of the Jewish army, Joshua remembers the oath sworn by the spies. Rahab and her family are saved; "she dwelt in Israel to this day." We do not know whether Salmon, who begat Boaz with Rahab, was one of the spies or met her at some later time. The text does not say. Given her previous life, she certainly did not become his wife. Nonetheless, Rahab's renown was not simply that she was an ancestor of David: Paul, in his Letter to the Hebrews, presents her as a great example of faith: "By faith Rahab the harlot did not perish with those who were disobedient, because she had given friendly welcome to the spies." The Church Fathers even see Rahab as a symbol of the Church, since by faith and love she preserved her family from annihilation; this shows how eagerly they took up the challenge to track and trace the history of salvation in every detail of the Old Testament.

Ruth appears as an example of pure gentleness and humility. She is a Moabitess, the widow of the Jew Mahlon; her mother-in-law, Naomi, who was married to Elimelech, is also a widow. Both women, now wretched and abandoned widows, have become beggars. Ruth gathers ears of grain from the fields of a rich relation of her husband's. His name is Boaz; he discovers the beautiful, demure grain-gleaner and shows favor to her. Accordingly, Ruth feels encouraged to wash, anoint herself, and put on her best clothes, and she goes literally to lie down in Boaz' bed. All this is completely honorable in the way it takes place, for she is asking him, since he is a relation of her husband's, to exercise his levirate duty. So Boaz proclaims at the gate of Bethlehem: "Ruth the Moabitess, the widow of Mahlon, I have bought to be my wife, to perpetuate the name of the dead in his inheritance, that the name of the dead may not be cut off from among his brethren." So Ruth becomes the mother of Obed, who will become the father of Jesse and grandfather of David.

The fourth woman in Jesus' family tree is Bathsheba, who was married to the Hittite captain Uriah. The story of how, one afternoon, King David gets up from his bed, goes for a walk on his roof terrace, and spies Bathsheba taking a bath on a neighboring roof has provided a wealth of material for artists, "for the woman was very beautiful". All the more infamously was Uriah dispatched. In a letter that has become legendary, David ordered a fatal attack, and the inconvenient husband was buried under a great heap of corpses; the death of so many was intended to cover up the murder of Uriah, who clearly suspected what had been going on. This event is followed by David's repentance and despair, a prayer that is heard by God, for Bathsheba becomes the mother of King Solomon, the fabulous Temple builder, the greatest Jewish king.

The adulteress, the prostitute, and the two aspiring, persistent widows were selected by the Evangelist Matthew as examples of exceptional women in the otherwise purely male family tree of the Redeemer. Many a preacher has found an edifying explanation for this somewhat unsettling selection. Some say that the Evangelist wanted to emphasize that Jesus' forebears were weak and culpable people; others suggest that it shows that Jesus, who saw himself as a "healer of the sick", was not afraid of being close to those burdened by sin; others, again, point to the fact that the Incarnation of the Son of God took place in the Bethlehem stable and in a family that was involved in sin in various ways. The idea sounds plausible; it has a nice Christian,

sentimental flavor to it. But does it fit in with the atmosphere of Matthew's Gospel with its laconic edge? The stains
on the House of David were painfully obvious to the Jewish author of this Gospel. What made this family special
was not its sinfulness, but the promise made to it from
Abraham's time, a promise that had been clarified and
renewed by the prophets. Jesus was to be the fulfillment of
this promise—but how could this come about if he were
not "David's son"?

Why does Matthew adjust his genealogy to fit in with magical numerology, omit the mention of three kings, and count
Jeconiah twice, in order to arrive three times at the numerical value of the name of David? And why does he make such
a startling selection of women? Are we not absolutely com-
pelled, on literary grounds, to see these women in connection with Mary, the last and most unknown of women,
the contemporary of Matthew, who deliberately introduces
her in the context of these famous historical women?

The first thing the four women in the genealogy of Jesus
have in common is that they are not Jewesses. Tamar and
Rahab actually come from peoples—Canaanites and citizens of the obliterated city of Jericho—held to be particularly wicked, even cursed. Initially, however, this common
feature does not bring us any farther with regard to Mary.
If it is meant to show that Mary, too, was a foreigner and
an outsider, it does not solve the riddle of Jesus' descent
from the House of David. Being a foreigner, coming from
a despised tribe, being graciously accepted into a nation
marked by the divine promise—none of this seems to mean
much for Mary if she was a Jewess and possibly even one of
David's descendants.

However, the four women have something else in common, something that may have occurred to the reader already:

all four were made pregnant by someone other than their husband. Bathsheba, the mother of Solomon, was "the wife of Uriah", and she stands in the genealogy under this title, not under her own name. This is the most important point. Rahab is a prostitute—her status is emphasized both in the Old Testament and in Saint Paul. By contrast Tamar and Ruth use schemes and pressure to get older relatives to give them children—which was entirely legal—for their dead husbands. So if Mary is to be compared to the four women, it is because she, too, did not get her son from her husband. All the offspring of the four women, the illegitimate and those legitimated by the levirate law, became "sons of Abraham" and members of the House of David. Powerful men stepped into the place of the husbands and raised up offspring in their name: the patriarch Judah, the victorious Salmon, the rich Boaz, and finally King David himself. Someone greater than Joseph, in Joseph's place, begat Mary's son, Jesus. In comparison with this Greater One, Mary was from a rejected and cursed generation, not from a particular people, but from the guilt-laden human race. By nature, therefore, Jesus is the Son of him who begot him, but according to the holy levirate law he is the son of Joseph, he is David's son and heir.

Mary, the new Rahab, rescues her people by faith in God's almighty power. As a new Tamar, she prevents her people from collapse and extinction. Ruth said to Boaz: "You are most gracious to me, my lord, for you have comforted me and spoken kindly to your maidservant", and Mary, the new Ruth, says in Saint Luke's Gospel: "My soul magnifies the Lord, and my spirit rejoices in God my Savior, for he has regarded the low estate of his handmaiden." As the new Bathsheba, Mary brings into the world a new Solomon, who, like the old Solomon, is a judge, but the Judge of the world.

If we were to imagine the four women of the genealogy as Romanesque or Gothic statues, they should really be carrying keys on their girdles, for it is they who unlock the family tree that can seem like a piece of ossified ceremonial. What at first seems like a genealogical register exhibiting the kind of contradictions that emerge when someone cheats at Patience is changed into a living message. Anyone who keeps reading and comes across Joseph's doubts when he learns that his betrothed is pregnant already knows what Joseph needs to hear from the mouth of the angel. In its indirect way, Matthew's genealogy of Jesus is the most comprehensive text about Mary to be found in the Gospels. Using the archaic means of a catalogue of generations, Matthew is expressing something utterly new, and in doing so he employs neither theological doctrine nor philosophy.

"In the beginning was the Word." So begins the Gospel of John. Matthew's beginning consisted of a chain of human beings disappearing into the darkness of the past. But something invisible was at work in this long human chain, giving direction to the merely biological sequence, imparting a forward thrust to it. We can only know this invisible reality and its effect if we read it in the faces of human beings. History, with its abstractions, is embodied in forms. These forms provide us with bundles of meanings, elucidated in turn by further forms. The reader is presented, not with a series of doctrinal statements, but with a sequence of people. Thus Matthew opens his account of the Word's Enfleshment with a sequence of human incarnations.

9

The Procession through the Sliding Door

A Passage from the Novel

A Long Night

"Don't listen to the priest when he speaks German. The priest is indispensable to the Mass, but he himself doesn't know how."

—*A Long Night*, chap. 5.

. . . It was dark when he went into the hotel. At the reception desk sat a worried-looking woman who gave him a suspicious glance. Herr Drais had already gone up, she said. It was the first time anyone had referred to Hermann as "Herr Drais". The building was from the fifties, when all Frankfurt's public buildings were floored with Solnhofer slate. A smell of soup wafted from the restaurant kitchen. The hotel was situated at the edge of a red-light district, but the belated modernity of its style, its insipid solidity—which it shared with many of the more recent church buildings—made one forget the surroundings.

The chapel was small, as understated as the hotel lobby. One concrete wall had circular, colored-glass windows. The pews were of yellow birchwood, and over the altar there was an aluminum crucifix with a cast figure made of red glass that recalled dried strawberry jam. The Virgin was represented as a sightless concrete cyclad. The room was hot under the sun's rays, and a smell of decay came from the flower vase on the altar. The autumn flowers had turned into a brownish pulp. Next to the vase stood a little silver cabinet adorned with lumps of rock crystal. As Ludwig entered, Hermann was in the process of getting rid of the flowers.

"Don't forget to genuflect in front of the silver tabernacle", Hermann whispered when he noticed Ludwig. He was glad he had come, but tense at the same time.

In the sacristy there was a plastic bottle with water in it. "Will you fill the basin by the door?" The basin was a glass dish in a brass holder that was encrusted with deposits. It could do with a cleaning first. Good that they had two hours to get ready. Everything on the altar had to be changed. At present it was covered with a piece of yellowish artificial velvet; to the left stood the silver tabernacle, and on the right there were two fat candles in ceramic saucers. It would all have to go. The tabernacle was moved to the center. Three very long, narrow linen cloths, starched and ironed, had to be spread over the altar so that they hung down to the floor to right and left. Ludwig and Hermann held these cloths between them and lowered them until they lay one on top of the other. Flanking the tabernacle Hermann placed six neo-Gothic bronze candlesticks, three on either side. Yellow candles were fixed in them: "yellow, not white!" said Hermann in a hushed voice. Then he took three cards out of a drawer, one wide and two narrower. The wide card had several columns of print on it, with the heading in red: "Canon missae". The narrow ones had a single column of print, headed "Lavabo" and "Initium"; the first of these was placed to the right, leaning against a candlestick, the second to the left, and the large one was set up in front of the silver cabinet. Now, not forgetting to genuflect, he placed a bronze bell on the stone step before the altar—or rather, a group of bells attached to one handle. The altar was ready.

At this point he turned his attention to the credence table, the little table near the sacristy door. He covered it with a white cloth. He picked up two strangely shaped glass jugs with high, narrow necks that would emit a fine stream. The jug without a handle was filled with water—not from the water bottle this time—and the jug with a handle was filled with wine from a bottle of Rheinhessen, a "dry late vintage", as it was described on the label. In this tubelike room the wine gave off a rather unpleasantly medicinal aroma. At the credence table Ludwig covered the little jugs with a starched linen cloth folded in three along its length. Next to it was placed a brass basin with a little brass jug—"water from the tap!"—and a small gold plate, newly resurfaced— "Don't touch it with your fingers: hold it with a white cloth!" Now the credence table was ready. Ludwig hoped he had put everything in the right place, arranging it all as symmetrically as possible, as on the altar. Hermann made no comment.

"Is there a red candle burning on the altar?" So that was where Hermann's red candle came from. No, there was no red candle on the altar. But on the sacristy table there were two. He lit one of them and put it, after making a genuflection, beside the silver cabinet.

"Now we can go into the sacristy."

Ludwig again felt that he was back with Hermann when they were children. Once again they were in a great game where every achievement led to further tasks. Hermann noticed—with sadness—that Ludwig did not like the chapel; everywhere he found something that betrayed lack of taste, and no doubt the chapel was indeed tasteless. So, where there was no beauty to distract them from imperfections of form, they had to follow the rules all the more strictly.

The next task was "the chalice". It was kept in a tall leather case. Ludwig opened it and saw a golden vessel with a tall foot, with a shallow golden plate in a little drawer below it. "You mustn't touch either chalice or paten. Lift them out with a white cloth." Hermann placed a folded cloth into the chalice so that its ends hung down on either side, then he covered it with the golden paten. Next he opened a wooden box and took out a large white wafer, stamped with grooves where it was to be broken. It was put on the paten, which in turn was covered by a stiff square card in an embroidered linen case. After that he looked in a deep drawer containing red, green, and violet brocades and pulled out a black one. It completely veiled the chalice and its superstructure. The roof of this arrangement was a square silk pouch containing a stiff, starched linen cloth. At this stage the chalice had become a tent of black brocade, its stiff black folds encompassing the vessel within.

The Mass garments, in the same colors as the silk cloths from the drawer, hung in a cupboard. Most of the vestments were nineteenth-century work. The colors were luminous; the fabric shone. They were rather worn in places, at the neck and shoulders. It was clear that these articles did not belong here. The black vestment hung there, too. Its brocade had a neo-Gothic motif. He laid it on the table, piling all manner of items on top of it: lengths of black silk brocade, linen smocks, cloths and girdles. Another task was complete.

Ludwig sat down on a bench. The chapel was still empty, but the red candle was burning. Daylight was fading. Now the chapel was ready; it was as bare and dreary as before, but its engine had started, so to speak. Although the sacristy door was closed, one could tell, Ludwig felt, that everything there was ready, too. He was grateful to Hermann for letting him help. He felt like a host expecting guests, surveying a table that was now set, with the bottles of red wine opened.

Bella had been in a friendly mood today, though a bit preoccupied; but there had been nothing cold about the look she gave him as he set off. Perhaps there was even the suggestion of a smile?

A man with a briefcase suddenly rushed in, glancing around in an attitude of puzzled irritation. His white hair, meticulously parted, made him look somewhat old-fashioned, like a military man. He seemed indignant, as if he were saying, "Are they at it again?" Then he saw Ludwig sitting on the bench. His face became even more set; he nodded to him as if he had just been given a slap on the back of his clean-shaven neck and hastily slipped past him. Then he stopped, looked back at Ludwig as if something had occurred to him, then slowly and solemnly genuflected in front of the silver cabinet.

Ludwig followed him into the sacristy. There he found the man already dressed in what looked like a white smock. Hermann was just hanging his jacket and striped tie on a coat hanger. The man was holding a thin piece of black cloth and trying to fix it around his neck like a bib. He managed it, with some difficulty. The upper part of the black bib held a yellowing band of celluloid and now proclaimed itself to be a clerical collar and stock.

"Are you attending this Mass?" The man jerked his head up in a gesture of alarm, simultaneously taking a step back in a birdlike combination of anger and caution. This was not a public Mass, he said. It was not forbidden to attend it, but it was intended to be kept for a small group. This Mass, he explained, was a special pastoral concession for a rather troublesome circle of believers. It was not for normal, instructed Catholics.

"This is not the core of the Church, if you understand what I am saying." Primarily it was intended for old people—"senior citizens"—the man said. Younger people did come as well, but that was a headache for him because this Mass was "quite clearly an obsolete model". The Church, he said, had rid itself, at long last, of the whole animistic, magical, ritual complex it had dragged along with it, for far too long, into the modern world. This gigantic burden—"a cathedral in a cart"—had isolated the Church from the great advances of modern intellectual life. Now there were just a few people left clinging to the old magical aspect of the Church, a tiny group, intellectually at a fairly low level, who could be ignored sociologically—but not, of course, pastorally. For decades these poor folk had had the fear of sin drummed into them, and now they had been left alone in the dark, as the new Church had discovered its path into the daylight. He was simply helping them to die.

"One has to be careful", he said, rotating his head and exercising his powerful arms. That was why he had half-strangled himself with his collar. "These people are much easier to lead if they have their priest with them." The bishop had no time for this kind of pastoral care; people were clamoring for him to write off these pig-headed ritualists. The bishop regarded this Mass, here on the hotel's second floor, as something "dangerous".

Hermann said nothing but went out with a cheerful look on his face. Ludwig introduced himself as Hermann's brother.

"I have a great regard for Herr Drais", the man said, as if he were making a risky assertion. Herr Drais' brother was obviously from the world of business; it was reassuring, and the man had the courage to be frank.

He indicated the Mass vestment laid out in readiness. "This black stuff—fortunately we have got rid of it everywhere. There was something of necrophilia about this gloomy funeral finery. Now at last we know the joy of being Christian." As he said this, his lips narrowed and his expression became more combative. Then he introduced himself: "Gessner", he said, offering Ludwig his vice-grip of a handshake. Ludwig felt obliged to return a firm masculine handshake. The man said he lectured in Church history at the university. Ludwig replied that he was in the wholesale business.

"The Church's wheels grind slowly", the professor said. "We are only beginning to adopt the achievements of the Reformation." Christianity, he said, originated in the Mediterranean area. Initially its rituals absorbed everything that was floating about in the great religious soup of Late Antiquity. Pagan elements, Roman Imperial cult, the cult of Mithras, of Isis, of Dionysus, Orphic cults, the Eleusinian mystery religion, the Platonic academy, the Jewish Temple cult, Jewish synagogue worship, early monastic customs (influenced by oriental ritual), Jewish, pagan, and Christian gnosticism: a fascinating brew from an archaeological point of view, but indigestible in terms of religion. Next, this vast swamp came under Roman rule. The Romans, with their Roman canon law, their rubrics, and their juridical categories, had drained this swamp, contained it, built dykes, and filled lakes, a whole lake-system, without having any feeling for what they were doing. Now that the mountain of rules, so exquisitely printed, had become so much trash, the fantastic, theatrical vestments had ended up in museums, the old rites had been abolished and were already thoroughly eradicated from the minds of Catholics—now everyone was gradually beginning to see and realize what had really been behind it all. The professor gave Ludwig a penetrating glance. His earlier, excited irritation had vanished. One could sense his glad anticipation as he prepared to tell this successful young man, set in the midst of the battle of modern life, something such a youth would never have expected to hear from a white-haired priest.

"We clerics have our secrets, but soon that will be all over. Priestcraft is finished. What was beneath this gigantic cultural rubbish heap, this giant liturgical wig? A bald pate, nothing. Or not much, at any rate. Or, at most, things that were vague, hard to grasp. The Last Supper—for that is what is supposed to be beneath the surface of the Latin ceremonial—what was it? We don't know. A sacrifice, as people are still happily parroting? A man has an evening meal with his friends—and that is supposed to be a sacrifice! You see, don't you, how the whole thing has been overloaded with that gruesome sacrifice theology and its Stone Age smell of blood. Just try to explain it to a non-Christian: God creates man, and man offends God so much that the only acceptable restitution is a superhuman sacrifice. So God allows his Son, in human form, to be barbarically slaughtered, and then he is satisfied and reconciled. Just you try it!"

"I cannot give you an answer, but I would like to know what my brother thinks", said Ludwig.

"Your brother would say it is a mystery", said the professor curtly, and went over to the washbasin. Hermann, he said, was so particular about every detail and would never fail to remind him, before they began to get dressed, "You must say the prayer Lavabo when washing your hands." He (the professor) would wash his hands anyway, because he had just come from the bus and they felt sticky. As for the prayer, however, he would leave it out because "by the time of Pius XII it was only optional, according to a decree of the Congregation of Rites." Hermann really ought to accept this, but he kept trying.

"He is stubborn and his own worst enemy", the professor said. "I could open doors for him. He could become a priest, a late vocation, in a very short time; I would be prepared to smooth his path, but he would have to wake up and finally get over his fixation on a hopeless cause. He may love it—I too love it—but it must become a Platonic love", he laughed noisily and grimly. Ludwig's school principal had laughed the same way; he had been a Protestant theologian: it was the laughter of bitter masculine theologians of all denominations, anxious to appear different from the others, sickly sweet and unctuous. Outside, Hermann had lit the candles. The front rows were occupied by three women with artificial fur hats, a blonde woman with two small children, an elderly man with one opaque lens in his glasses, an irritable-looking red-faced man, an impeccably coifed pale woman with a finely shaped nose, and an unshaven man who was confusedly leafing through one of the black books that had been provided. Eventually perhaps thirty people had assembled. Ludwig tried to discover some common denominator among them, waiting there in quiet expectation, but he failed. It was as if thirty people waiting at a bus stop had been brought here. Finally a bell rang, the sacristy door opened, and everyone stood up: Ludwig felt a momentary sense of real surprise, in spite of having spent some time in the anteroom.

They say that, at the fall of Constantinople, the city's entire civilian population gathered in Hagia Sophia, where an uninterrupted series of Masses was offered to implore a miracle of deliverance. Here, at their most sacred place, which until then had been a refuge for the persecuted, the Greeks had to submit to the annihilation of all hope, the desecration of all the sanctuaries hitherto so religiously preserved, as well as their own extermination and demise. A story was passed on among the survivors to the effect that when the Turks broke in, an angel opened a crack in the wall and led the celebrating priests out through it. One day, it was said, the wall would open again at the same point and admit into the Temple those who had been thus kept safe for the future day of salvation. Ludwig, who for the most part remembered only anecdotes from the history books he read, had retained this image of the crack in the wall and the procession disappearing into it—to reappear at a later date—as an expression of a hope against all reason, against all appearances, against all the laws of history; now, as the sliding door rumbled open, it was as if the moment, so longed for by the unfortunate Greeks, had come, only the procession had got lost and, instead of arriving in Istanbul at Hagia Sophia, it had found its way into this bare anteroom. Hermann was now wearing a black soutane that reached down to the ground and, over it, a knee-length white linen surplice trimmed with lace at neck and hem. It made him look surprisingly childlike and clean, as if he were about to be baptized. After him came Professor Gessner, a little black rimless hat on his head, with a deep red silk pompom on it; he was wearing all the garments that Ludwig and Hermann had laid out in layers, one on top of the other. Thus they proceeded through the pews until they reached the altar. There they formed up and genuflected. A bearded man at the little organ began a long chant in his bass voice. The professor held out his hat to Hermann, who kissed his hand as he took the hat from him. Then the professor, remaining in a deep bow, began a lengthy, whispered dialogue with Hermann, kneeling beside him, while both of them beat their breasts. While this was going on the bearded man sang a convoluted melody in a minor key; it changed into a psalm-chant and then back again. These chants were reminiscent of oriental, Arabic, or Indian music. Sometimes the people in the pews would sing with him, and then Professor Gessner, in his strained and unattractive voice, would sing something from a huge book on the black-covered lectern. As he did this his face was not visible: he stood with his back to the people, turning around only occasionally, his head bowed and his arms open, showing the palms of his hands, engaging in a kind of formalized dialogue with the congregation. His movements were stiff and jerky, like a clockwork puppet. It was clear throughout that he was not at ease with what he was doing, that he was acting under some constraint.

Ludwig was puzzled at this, but he supposed that these automatic movements were what Hermann was expecting. Nothing indicated that what was taking place had anything to do with Professor Gessner's personality, preferences, or intellect. He was obliged to suppress his irascibility and impatience for the duration of these events. It was as if he had to conceal his indignant, energetic features while the Mass was going on. Now the bearded man was singing a long chant with many short verses, carried along, as it were, by the melody: the singer's white, moon face was staring, his eyes protruding a little. He looked like a sculpted figure on a fountain; the music flowed from his mouth in an endless song like a stream of water, followed by a longer croaking chant from Gessner, this time on the left side of the altar.

Hermann had told Ludwig that he was better off know-ing nothing. "Hermann is my pope", Ludwig smiled to himself, politely declining the black book, opened at the page, that his neighbor pushed toward him. Yet his inno-cence had already taken a blow when, in connection with these rites, Professor Gessner had talked about the idea of "sacrifice" as the height of nonsense. As luck would have it, no harm had been done. The theological dispute out-lined polemically by Gessner—who took Ludwig for a Cath-olic well versed in these issues—did not touch him. What *did* affect him, and in a special way, was the realization that he had actually just participated in a "sacrifice".

As Gessner had pointed out, sacrifice was by and large a bloody business. The Persian king used to kill a beauti-ful horse in sacrifice every morning. On Aztec pyramids selected young persons, dressed in shimmering garments of colored feathers, had their hearts cut from their living bodies in sacrifice to powerful deities. The Greeks sacri-ficed oxen, the Romans sheep or rams; Socrates sacrificed a cockerel. Nowadays people killed in an accident are called "victims" [German: "sacrifices"]. "An accident on a round-about claimed one victim"—that was how Fidi's death had been announced in the newspaper. Was Fidi a "victim", or was this only the witless terminology of a time that knows nothing of sacrifice and victim? Ludwig thought about the picture Bella had described to him: Fidi, with-out a mark on him, asleep, naked, on a high bed under a bright light, his breathing sustained through slender tubes, his corpse supplied with ineffectual substances. Their father also lay on a high bed, but there was no bright light, and he did not lie stretched out, but curled up like a worm. When Ludwig struggled with the stiff-starched and ironed altar cloths, carefully laying them on top of each other, was it not as if he were helping to change his father's bed linen?

Then it had been their father lying in this white bed, in that new kind of immobility that is so incomprehensibly different from the lack of movement of a living person. In this room, filled with sunlight, the smoke of incense and singing, he was reminded of what Pressler had said: "The two things I say most often are, 'I don't understand it', and 'That's quite simple.'" Ludwig could have said both at the same time, for, on the one hand, he understood nothing, in fact, of what had been going on in front of him; and yet at the same time he felt an idea welling up within him—it was suddenly compelling, something utterly evident and very simple: on the altar's white cloths lay his father and Fidi and perhaps even more of the dead, but their bodies were small and the black shape of Professor Gessner's back completely obscured them.

Now it was quiet. Everyone was kneeling, and Professor Gessner was whispering, turning pages in the Missal, and Hermann in his soutane was kneeling beside him, the bell in one hand while, with the other, he held the chasuble up a little. Professor Gessner bent forward and whispered a little more distinctly, then genuflected; the little bell was rung, and he lifted a little, white, round wafer high in the air while the bell rang three times, and Ludwig forgot that Hermann had taken the wafer from the wooden box and put it on the little golden plate on top of the chalice. This white disc in a cloud of incense—he did not see it as something material at all, or rather, he saw it, for one moment, as something very fine and delicate, like solidified light. Then the hands came down and Professor Gessner started reading in a whisper again. . . .

10

Revelation through Veiling in the Old Roman Catholic Liturgy

In the books of the old rite, which were normative until the liturgical reform, to veil something is to reveal it: it is revelation through veiling.

At the beginning of this rite the celebrant is veiled: he is clothed with garments that all have a symbolic character. First the celebrant puts the amice over his head while reciting a prayer that speaks of the helmet of God; but the chief veiling here is a gesture that is even more expressive in pagan and Jewish antiquity: it signifies repentance and mourning as well as reverence for the holy place. It is striking that the attributes and virtues such as chastity, fortitude, and humility, associated with the various vestments in short prayers, are really regarded as parts of that "armor of God" about which Saint Paul talks.

Quite literally, the new Man, Christ, is "put on". Of course the prayer also expresses the wish that this outward clothing be followed by an inner transformation, but the outward act remains essential: grace comes "from above", which means from outside. Man regards the process of his perfecting, not as his own achievement, but as a gift that he receives from outside and makes his own by clothing himself with it. In the case of a bishop, even his hands and feet are clothed; he is completely "packaged up", and it always makes me think of Mircea Eliade's description of those African tribal priests who have to be carried everywhere, lest they lose any of their sacral power through contact with the ground. Of course there is no reference to this aspect in the liturgical books. The liturgical prescriptions of the West studiously avoid any reference to mystical and sacral ideas. A decidedly sober rationalism informs Western liturgical literature, an express not-wanting-to-know; this is the great historico-religious background against which the individual liturgical requirement is made. Right at the beginning of Christianity, visible in the conflict between Peter and Paul, there were very different attitudes to paganism. On the one hand, there was a strict, puritanical rejection of any connection between the "pagan abominations" and the new faith; and, on the other hand, there was a universalist attitude that saw paganism as a second Old Testament, in which the Holy Spirit had prepared the way, through art and philosophy, for the coming of the Redeemer. For this latter tradition, the fact that the Catholic priesthood preserved elements of priesthood of all times was entirely natural; for the former tradition, it was suspect and odious. At all events, the bishop's fullness of priestly, consecratory power is expressed with particular clarity when he puts on his vestments, recapitulating the various degrees of ordination: he wears the subdeacon's tunicle, the deacon's dalmatic, and the priestly chasuble on top of each other. When he comes to the sacramental act and takes the Host in his hands, he takes off his gloves, allowing full freedom, as it were, to the current of consecration he himself has received through the imposition of hands.

The bishop's procession is accompanied by altar servers wearing large cloths called *velum* on their shoulders; their task is to hold the episcopal insignia, miter, and crozier during the liturgy. These veils conceal the servers' hands; at one time even the Book of the Gospels was carried by hands concealed under the Mass vestments. The veiling of hands is an ancient gesture of reverence on the part of servants. Even in modern times, in a secular context, servants waiting at table used to wear white gloves: this was a faint and fading echo of the terrifying archangels before the throne of God, as described in the Apocalypse of Saint John, using three pairs of wings to hide their hands, feet, and faces.

The Apocalypse is the New Testament's liturgical book. Veiled like the angels, the altar servers surround the sacrificial priest who is to perform the slaughter of the Lamb. At the Offertory—the beginning of the sacrificial action, following the readings of Scripture and the Creed—the subdeacon carries the sacrificial implements and gifts to the altar. The chalice is covered with the paten, on which the Host lies. It in turn is covered by a stiffened linen lid, the pall, and over everything there is a large cloth, also called a "veil", of the same color as the other vestments. The veiled chalice thus looks like a tent; it is a miniature "tabernacle", that is, the Ark of the Covenant, containing the holy vessels. The subdeacon has a large veil put around his shoulders and carries the chalice with the Host hidden inside it. Thus the sacrificial gift, as yet unconsecrated, is honored by the same veiling as the consecrated gift at a later stage, for the communion chalice, the ciborium with the consecrated Hosts, is also carried beneath a veil. It is no different in the Eastern Church: here too, at the procession of the sacrificial gifts prior to the Consecration, the bread destined and ready for the sacrifice and the wine are hidden under veils as they are brought forward for the people's veneration. The veiled sacrificial gift is Christ prior to his crucifixion, not yet offered up; it is not yet the sign of contradiction, lifted high up; it is also the clothed Christ, waiting to be stripped of his garments.

Once the subdeacon has brought the sacrificial gifts and vessels to the altar, the deacon hands the paten to him. At this point the subdeacon goes to take his place on the altar steps, holding the paten up in front of him, veiled by the humeral veil. Two different things have been seen in this gesture. First, it is an act of reverence for the plate that is destined to bear the consecrated Host, the Body of the Lord. Second, however, it is an ancient Roman custom. In the first century the pope used to send particles of the Host from his own Mass to all the city's station-churches. The subdeacon, veiled, is thought to have carried these particles in front of him on the paten, showing that the Mass that had just been celebrated was linked to the Mass of the pope, the Church's visible head. It also showed that, because of the suspension of time and history that takes place in every offering of the Mass, there was only one sacrifice, Christ's sacrifice on Golgotha, from which all liturgical sacrifice proceeds and to which all liturgical sacrifice returns. So this angel, bearing the Lamb that was slain, highly lifted up in the veiled sacrificial vessel, was an embodiment of the eternal liturgy that the Apocalypse calls the "marriage of the Lamb", on which all earthly liturgies, if they do what they are intended to, are simply dependent.

At the time the rite was being shaped, this veiling of the paten was also adopted into the simpler forms of Mass, because it was held to be so important. If there is no subdeacon at the liturgy, during the Offertory the priest pushes the paten underneath the "corporal", the square cloth on which the Host, the "Body of Christ", lies. These and other actions at the altar are concealed from the congregation; they are hidden by the priest's body, which serves as a living iconostasis. The fact that certain actions and gestures are hidden from sight is also a deliberate veiling. The Eastern Church's wall of icons does this; its counterpart in the Western millennium are the high choir return stalls, altars remote from the people, and "ciborium altars" that can be entirely hidden behind curtains; even today, in Rome, many of these stone baldachinos over the altar reveal the curtain rails and bronze curtain rings of late antiquity. In the West, in the old rite, all that remained of this veiling were the communion rails (themselves a shrunken form of the altar enclosure) and, occasionally, the significant distance between altar and congregation; but the celebrants' backs, clothed in vestments of the same color, also formed a wall in front of the sacrificial action. Three strands of tradition are twisted together in this veiling. First there is the Jerusalem Temple with its curtain veiling the Holy of Holies. In front of this curtain incense was burned on the altar of incense, while the holocaust offerings were burned on the altar of whole burnt offerings; thus in Jerusalem the sacrifice took place in front of the curtain. The invisible God, symbolized by the incense, remained hidden inside the Holy of Holies. This curtain also appealed to the pagan liturgical imagination. In Hellenistic times it was stolen from the Temple—it was colored with Phoenician purple and of the most precious workmanship—and placed in the Temple of Zeus of Olympia, in the *cella* in front of the huge statue of Zeus. It could be lowered from the ceiling into a chest decorated with ebony reliefs at the statue's feet.

This innovation in the Temple of Zeus—for the Greek image of the god did not actually need such veiling, since the *cella* was always shut, except for very few festival days—brings us to the second strand of tradition in the Christian liturgy's practice of veiling and concealing. The ritual of the epiphany of the monarch was known from the court of the Persian *basileus*; Diocletian eventually introduced it into the court of the Roman emperor. On particular days the court assembled in the imperial aula to venerate the emperor and his family. The imperial family gathered ahead of time behind a closed curtain; when the curtain opened, the court fell to their knees in "prostration". In Byzantine iconography these curtains became an important element in the portrayal of saints: the saint appears in the icon between two parted curtains—this is the moment of the saint's epiphany, to which those who behold it respond by veneration. In the liturgy, too, as a result of the veiling of the rite, new instances of epiphany are always occurring—the Word of God, carried in procession from the sanctuary, the Offertory gifts, carried in procession or, when transformed into the Lord's Body, lifted up above the priest's head to be shown to the faithful (in the Western rite).

The third strand of tradition has not, in my view, been generally acknowledged, although it is an old and familiar custom. Since the earliest times Masses have been celebrated at the Holy Sepulchre, not only in the body of the church of the Holy Sepulchre with its many altars, but also in the burial chamber itself. Priest and faithful assemble in the grave's antechamber and recite the readings that precede the sacrifice. Then the priest enters the burial chamber, where he uses the grave's niche as an altar; the grave cloths become a kind of altar cloth. Once inside, he cannot be seen by the congregation, who remain in the antechamber. They only hear his voice. The Consecration that takes place in the hidden space of the grave unites the sacrificial act of Golgotha and the moment of Resurrection inside the grave, for this Resurrection was also a kind of transubstantiation; it was the greatest step any substance can undergo: from death to life. The faithful who stand facing the choir-screen, the iconostasis, or the priest's back that hides the action from them are, as it were, standing outside the grave in Jerusalem. Here, in utter seclusion, without human witnesses, the Resurrection took place. The Church of the Holy Sepulchre in Jerusalem was the first church to be founded by Emperor Constantine; ecclesiastical architecture begins with the building of this church. When Constantine's mother, Helen, discovered the Cross, there began a period of reconstruction of the history of Jesus' sufferings, in which the details of the grave—faith's center and focus—were of course studied with particular diligence.

Prior to the Offertory in the Eastern Church the deacon cries out, "The doors, the doors! Attend to the doors!" This is all that remains of the ritual of concealment in the Eastern Church. In the Western Church we have the lowest degree of the clerical state, the *ostiarius*, the doorkeeper, whose responsibility was to make sure that, after the readings of Scripture, neither the unbaptized nor public sinners took part in the sacrificial mystery. In the first century, on the basis of the apostles' teaching and practice, the liturgy was understood as the celebration of a mystery—where outsiders and the uninitiated had no business. They belonged in the narthex, the church's anteroom, where the priest absolved the penitent with the stroke of a long staff; the name of this staff was *narthex*, and it was given to this hall, where those excluded from the mysteries had to remain. Staffs of this kind were still in use in Rome, in the seven main basilicas, up to the Council and even after it. In Latin these staffs are called *vindicta*. In antiquity the praetor freed a slave by touching him with a staff of this kind; so the confessor freed people from the *slavery of sin* and *subjection to the law* by touching them with the staff. We can see how rapidly Roman juridical thought and sacramental thought fused into one in the mind of a Paul. In later centuries, when it was no longer possible to ascertain the fitness of the members of the congregation to participate in the celebration, it was still felt necessary to protect the cultic mysteries from being profaned. In the second Christian millennium, in the West, we find the beginnings of the custom of whispering the most sacred formulae, the "Canon", with its high point in transubstantiation, thus concealing it behind a veil of silence.

The golden receptacle in which the Hosts remaining after the Communion are kept is called the "tabernacle", after the Ark of the Covenant in the Mosaic Temple. Tabernacle means "tent", which suggests something made of cloth. The tabernacle doors are hidden behind brocade curtains, usually in the liturgical colors. The only color forbidden on the tabernacle is black, which is reserved for the Mass of the Dead and Good Friday: it would contradict the presence of the living God. Most tabernacles have a further curtain inside, and each of the ciboria, the vessels containing the Hosts, is also covered with a coatlike veil. Taking a ciborium from the tabernacle is like peeling an onion: behind each layer one finds another.

Finally let us mention the veiling that, for most people, is the most striking and familiar instance of liturgical veiling: the veiling of the crosses and holy images from Passion Sunday until Good Friday. This veiling occurs in Lent, when the liturgy is celebrated with a certain leanness. The organ is silent, as are the bells from Holy Thursday to Good Friday; certain prayers are not said; and the altar may not be decorated with flowers. This veiling of the images and crosses is thus sometimes called a "fasting of the eyes". However, it is not actually intended as a withdrawal of the appeal to the senses. Rather, it comes from the cult that surrounded the authentic Cross of Christ that Empress Helen found in Jerusalem, the *vera crux* in Jerusalem and subsequently in Rome, in the Church of Santa Croce in Gerusalemme. Like every relic, the holy Cross was wrapped in cloths and spent the year in the sacristy. On Good Friday it was brought into the church and unpacked in a solemn ritual so that it could be shown to the faithful. Two deacons, one on either side, watched over the Cross, to make sure that the faithful, coming forward to kiss the Cross, resisted the temptation to steal a splinter from it. These splinters also reached many European centers legally. The Enlightenment's mocking suggestion that, if all the fragments of the Cross, scattered far and wide and preserved in beautiful ostensories, were collected, they would make an entire forest has no basis in reality; it has been calculated that this hypothetical reassembly of fragments would produce no more than a large beam of timber—which, of course, says nothing about the authenticity of the individual relics of the Cross. At all events, the splinters of the Cross were treated the same in Europe as in Jerusalem and Rome: in France and Germany, too, the fragments were solemnly unpacked in front of the congregation, to be venerated. In the end this cult was adopted by communities that had no relic of the Cross: the cross above the altar was taken down and wrapped up, to be venerated on Good Friday in the same way as the *vera crux*, as we have described. Here the purpose of the veiling was not to withdraw the cross from sight: it was so that the cross would be treated like the real Cross; from being a devotional object, a cultic object, a sacred symbol, it would once again become the real instrument of torture on which Christ died. Thus we see that the veiling of the crosses is intended only to stress the historical nature of the work of Redemption, just as the name of Pontius Pilate—that modestly successful provincial administrator—is used in the Creed: it speaks of the real death on a real cross in a concrete place at a precisely identifiable hour of world history. It is designed to contradict the mythical, allegorical, symbolic interpretation of the events portrayed in the New Testament.

For "Enlightenment" movements of all ages, this religious practice of veiling is the very epitome of obscurantism. Just as the concept of "illuminism" puts forward the idea of a bright light, shining into a dark cellar full of spiders' webs and rats, the Enlightenment rhetoric likes to see itself tearing down veils and destroying masks. What the veil concealed from the pious was merely a deception. It was a distinct handicap that Baroque allegories portrayed "Fides" as a woman with her veil drawn down over her eyes. (There may have been a subversive intention here; the question would need to be examined.) Faith, these pious people said, is a free and deliberate blindness—not exactly a metaphor attracting imitation. It was a defensive approach to faith, distorted by the hostility of rationalism; it was felt necessary to associate religion with a *sacrificium intellectus*. In fact, the meaning of the cultic veil had been clear to believers since the most ancient times. When Pompey entered the Jerusalem Temple as conqueror, he pulled aside the Temple veil—a sacrilegious act that scandalized the priests. What he saw filled him with a great sense of triumph, a feeling very familiar to us. Behind the veil there was nothing at all.

The extension of the practice of veiling to all the crosses in a church, and to its images and statues, is of a later date. It has nothing to do with the veiling of the Cross on Good

Friday. Latin Christendom's encounter with the Byzantine Church during the Crusades created the need to adapt the idea of the iconostasis, at least for the Lenten period. In Cluny, in Lent, they began enclosing the altar area with huge painted Lenten cloths. During Lent the cult took place hidden behind this cloth wall. In Germany some of these huge Lenten cloths have been preserved, notably in Zittau and Brandenburg. After the Council of Trent the custom of veiling the rites declined rapidly in Europe. What remained was the practice of veiling the images and statues. This had the effect of transforming the entire church into a narthex, an unadorned anteroom where, according to the custom of the ancient Church, public sinners would wait to be absolved. According to the reform of Cluny, the whole community was to regard itself as doing penance, like public sinners, and was to remain outside the sanctuary until Easter.

But, to return to the Temple: What should have been behind the veil? Did Pompey really believe that, by interfering with their sanctuary, he had lit a lamp for believing Jews? What he did not see, or did not want to see, was this: the curtain did not veil the message; the curtain contained the message that animated the Temple worshippers.

The real meaning of veiling is given to us by the earliest mention of a veiling—a covering—that we find in Holy Scripture. After the Fall, Adam and Eve discovered to their horror "that they were naked", and they made clothes from leaves. There is something profoundly disturbing about this passage, for, according to the teaching of Genesis, man was created perfect; his nakedness was, not a defect, but an expression of his likeness to God. After the breaking of God's command, the defect is suddenly there, although man remains outwardly unchanged. He has lost something; it is not there, and it awakens a sense of loss within him. Theology calls this defect the loss of grace. Man clumsily tries to make up for this loss. He puts clothes on to try to regain the radiance that had formerly surrounded him.

Veiling, therefore, becomes a visible sign of the nimbus of grace and holiness that has become invisible to human eyes. Veiling, in the liturgy, is the halo that is by nature appropriate to the sacred vessels and their even more sacred contents. This must never be forgotten if these vessels, signs, and Hosts are to be correctly understood. Veiling, in the liturgy, is not intended to withdraw some object from view, to make a mystery out of it, or to conceal its appearance. The appearance of the veiled things is common knowledge anyway. But their outward appearance tells us nothing about their real nature. It is the veil that indicates this. If one draws this veil aside, and the veils that lie behind it, like peeling an onion, and penetrates to the core of the mystery, one is still confronted with a veil: the Host itself is a veil, as a French hymn says: "O divine Eucharistie, o trésor mystérieux / Sous les voiles de l'hostie est caché le roi des Cieux."

If one wanted to formulate a theological doctrine of the veil, one could say that God's creation is real, but this reality, this ability to be real, is weakened because of original sin. Its lack of reality, its lost ability to radiate beyond itself and manifest itself as the Creator's thought is designated by the veil that represents this radiance.

In the new rite introduced by Pope Paul VI, and the practical implementation that went far beyond it (often with episcopal encouragement), the custom of veiling has disappeared almost entirely. No longer is there a distinction between sanctuary and congregation, particularly in new churches, and in old churches the obliteration of this distinction has often involved barbaric damage to the church's artistic form. There is no longer the veil of silence during the Canon, nor are the sacred vessels and ciboria veiled any more. The office of subdeacon, attested from the third century, has been abolished. The rite of the veiled paten no longer exists, either. One still finds the humeral veil being used for Benediction—the sacramental blessing with the monstrance—but Benediction itself has become a rare occurrence. Veiling the cross in Passiontide is now a matter of choice; in some places it is done, in others not.

The argument given for the liturgical reform is always that it has liberated the rite of Mass from all later accretions and "restored" it to the "purest" possible form, closer to that of primitive Christianity. In this context, veils and veiling are held to be instances of these "later accretions", although in fact they are signs of the mystery character the liturgy had in those first centuries. Liturgical archaeologism, like all forms of historicism and restorationism—in the world of art, too—falls under the accusation Faust makes against his acquaintance, Wagner, drunk with too much history: "Call it you may 'the spirit of the times': / It is the spirit of the powerful, to which the times must bend."

In this context, a liturgy that renounces all veiling has nothing to say. Presenting us with nothing but naked materiality, it takes account neither of creation's supernatural perfection nor of the world's need of redemption.

Appendix 1

"This Is My Body"

On Veneration of the Sacrament of the Altar in the Catholic Church

I would like to tell you about the sacred Host, how I came into contact with it, and what this contact has taught me. As a child, initially, I saw the Host only from a great distance. I saw priests and levites moving to and fro, dressed in gold-embroidered garments; I saw them bowing, offering incense; I heard them singing and speaking. Suddenly the church, full of people and resounding with the music of the organ, fell quiet: the priest bent forward over the altar; from his posture it was clear that he was doing something up there, but his back hid it from view. At the same time the levites and servers were on their knees, one could hear the silvery tinkling of a little bell, and then the great church bells in the tower began to speak. Ponderously at first, these giant pieces of cast metal started swinging, producing a dizzying, unrhythmical din that seemed to invest the entire air limitlessly, gradually settling down into a regular peal. The server with the thurible put more grains of incense from the silver vessel (called the "boat") onto the glowing coals, and dense white clouds arose, spreading out into the whole sanctuary area, so that the air swam. Then the priest stood up straight again, and, in this bluish, smoke-filled air that transformed the rays of the morning sun into something material, he lifted a small white disc high above his head. The people in the church knelt, many beat their breasts, others bowed their heads as if they dared not behold the white disc, others crossed themselves as if they needed additional protection in the face of what was confronting them. The silence continued even after this elevation of the Host. The bells slowed their tempo and faded away. But the silence had woven a powerful spell; it was only broken by a further ringing of the little silver bell, at which the people stood up and prayed quietly with the priest at the altar as, with arms outstretched, he sang the *Pater noster*.

The Privilege of Touching the Sacred Vessels

As a diminutive altar boy I had opportunity to deepen this impression. In the sacristy I watched the old sacristan, whose son had by now relieved him of many duties, as he pre-pared the sacred vessels for the altar sacrifice. He took the richly decorated chalice out of its little cylindrical leather case; the chalice had an especially broad foot to prevent it from being easily overturned, and its tapering neck had a bulbous part called the *nodus*, as I learned, below the cup (*coppa*). I had already observed, from a distance, that the priest, after lifting up the Host, kept his thumb and fore-finger together while praying. The "master of ceremonies" turned the pages of the Missal so that the priest did not have to separate these two fingers.

The outer end of the key to the tabernacle was wide and flat, so that the priest could hold the key between forefin-ger and middle finger when opening the little golden chest to remove the ciborium containing the Hosts for the congregation. The chalice's *nodus* also enabled him to hold the chalice without parting his thumb and forefinger at the ritual elevations and when receiving Communion himself. The old sacristan told me: "The priest must not touch anything else with his fingers that have touched the sacred Host until he has washed these fingers with water and wine over the chalice after giving Communion and drunk this mixture of water and wine that contains particles from the Host." The sacristan enjoyed a significant privilege for a layman: he was allowed to touch the sacred vessels; the bishop himself had given permission. His son, however, was not allowed. If his son had to fetch the chalice, he had to put on white gloves, as he did when he brought the heavy monstrance from the cupboard (his father could no longer lift it).

The sacristan, for his part, dealt with the altar linen. He took the cloth the priest had used to wipe the chalice after Communion, which was now moist with the wine that had been transformed into the Precious Blood, and rinsed it in a bowl of water. This bowl was emptied into the *sacrarium*, a drain situated behind the altar, communicating directly with the earth. He did the same with the "corporal", the square linen cloth kept in a brocade purse ("burse") in the liturgical color of the particular feast; this corporal was so called because the *Corpus Christi*, the consecrated Host, lay upon it. The point of this is that there must be no possibility of even a tiny fragment of the transubstantiated gifts being dishonored. The corporal was stiffly starched so that it was almost like cardboard. When the priest opened it out, the sharp folds created a platelike depression that prevented any particles that might break off from the Host from being swept away and falling to the ground.

Similar attention was given to the distribution of Communion. People knelt at rails that separated the sanctuary from the nave and were covered with a white cloth. They folded their hands under the cloth; if a Host were to fall during the distribution, it would fall onto this cloth. In addition, the priest giving Communion was accompanied by a server carrying a small gold plate, the "paten", held under the chin of each communicant. The priest would carefully examine this paten for particles when rinsing the chalice and washing his fingers after the Communion.

I learned that everyone wishing to receive Communion had to prepare himself for it. So that the Lord's Body should be clearly distinct from "common food", as the Apostle Paul says, it was to be received on an empty stomach. Priests had to fast from midnight if they were to celebrate Mass in the morning. Laymen had been excluded from this rule since Pius XII: they needed to fast for only three hours prior to Communion; but of course, if they were going to Mass at eight or nine in the morning, it mostly came to the same thing as the old rule. That custom has entered into many languages: in English "breakfast" and French "*déjeuner*", the word actually means "breaking the fast" and refers to the end of the eucharistic fast, that is, after Mass.

No doubt the high point of adoration of the Host was the Feast of Corpus Christi. It was intended to be a celebration of the mystery of Holy Thursday, but a joyful and triumphant celebration, without the veil of sadness of Christ's impending Passion. Christ the King, having triumphed over death, was to go in procession through the town. An especially large Host was consecrated so that it could be clearly visible in the monstrance behind the crystal panes of the sunburst. The procession adopted the sign language of medieval protocol for a king entering his city. The consecrated

Host was treated like a monarch. The procession path was strewn with flower petals and carpets. Just as a king traveling over land merited the use of a baldachino as a mark of his status, a baldachino or canopy was always carried above the Host once the priest, carrying it, had left the church. To carry the baldachino was an honor. When I was a child, prominent men of the community, in morning dress and with white gloves, used to carry the baldachino, and servers walked beside it with the silver bells I have mentioned, ringing them continuously so that the people standing along the street could be aware of the approaching Sacrament: when it came into view, they would fall to their knees in adoration. There were special rules for kneeling. The reserved Sacrament (consecrated Hosts kept in the church's tabernacle for the sick, with a red lamp burning day and night to signify what the tabernacle contained) was saluted by a genuflection of the right knee. The Host in the monstrance, on the other hand, which stood on the altar at Benediction and was carried through the streets at Corpus Christi, was honored by kneeling on both knees and bowing one's head.

As an altar server I also saw the Host close up. There was a slight sheen on the round wafer. It often had an image embossed on it, a crucifix, a chi-rho, or, at Christmas, a little Baby Jesus, tightly wrapped in swaddling clothes. Also, the priest's Host had break-marks scored in it so that when it was broken it did not make a lot of splinters and crumbs that would be hard to gather up. After the priest had uncovered the Host at the Offertory, that is, when he removed the brocade veil and the pall (the stiffened linen lid) from the golden paten that carried the Host and gave the paten to the subdeacon—who held it up, hidden beneath a large humeral veil, for the duration of the Offertory—the Host lay on the starched linen corporal. The priest stood before it with both hands raised and looked down at this white disc on the white cloth. When he touched it, he always used both hands. He covered it with a great number of signs of the cross; he could not speak to it, or about it, without constantly blessing it; and of course these blessings over the consecrated Host were intended not so much to bless the Host as to express the blessing that now emanated from it.

Most of the Forms of Reverence Have Disappeared

I always found it embarrassing to see the Host at such close quarters, so vulnerable, as if it were lying naked on the white cloth. It was not something for my eyes, a layman's eyes, to behold. There was something secret going on between the priest and the Host. It was a real relationship: there was a kind of conversation between Host and priest that was hidden from the eyes of the congregation by the priest's body. I, however, as an altar server, was aware and had to be aware of it, like a nurse who unexpectedly finds herself in the position of having to undress a respected personage. The gentle cracking sound the Host made when it broke seemed not for my ears, either: it was an intimacy to which I was not entitled.

It is generally known that, since Vatican II, much has changed in the Catholic Church with regard to this veneration of the Host (which means "sacrificial gift" in Latin). Most of the forms of reverence I have described have disappeared. The liturgical reformers succeeded in convincing the faithful that reverence for the Host, worship of the Host as the real physical appearance of Jesus Christ, had been unknown in the Church of the apostles and their early successors. This veneration of the Host was medieval, they said.

The word "medieval" has an even more pejorative sound in the modern Church than it has in modern philosophy and historiography, where people are at last beginning to question the idea of the "darkness of the Middle Ages"— that favorite Enlightenment cliché. In fact, as this "medieval" darkness starts to lighten and dissipate, we begin to discern the profile of one of the most creative, most multifaceted, and richest periods of human history—and one of the most adventurous in spiritual terms.

However, my concern today is not to correct our view of the Middle Ages. In my search for an uninterrupted tradition of authentic liturgy, I discovered the services of the Eastern Church. Here I paid special attention to the veneration offered to the Host, for the Eastern Church's liturgy cannot in any way be associated with the Middle Ages: its unchanged tradition, coming from the early part of the first millennium, is dogmatically beyond question. For the Byzantine Christian, liturgy is a revelation of God, given to man from above; God, worshipped and served by cherubim and seraphim, gives men the grace to participate in this angelic worship and approach him. It is strictly forbidden to change or adapt this divine liturgy: to do such a thing would also conflict with the way the participants understand their role in the liturgy.

The Eastern Church's Sacramental Practice

In the Byzantine world the Hosts look different from those in the West. Whereas the Latin Church uses unleavened bread in imitation of the Jewish usage of the Pasch, the Eastern Church holds to Christ's assertion that he is the leaven and accordingly regards leavened bread as alone appropriate—a practice the Western Church fully respects as a specific tradition, just as it respects all other divergences in the Eastern practice of the sacraments. In Ernst Benz' celebrated book on the Eastern Church, I read that the Eastern Church does not practice veneration of the Host to the same extent as the Western. Benz states that there is no eucharistic worship, no Benediction of the Blessed Sacrament, and no tabernacle in the Eastern Church. His book is remarkable in many ways, but at this point I felt I could detect a Protestant admirer of Orthodoxy trying to distance the Eastern Church as far as possible from the Latin Church.

My own experiences in the Greek, Russian, and Coptic liturgies confirmed this impression. *Of course* the Orthodox Church has tabernacles for the reserved Sacrament. At the conclusion of the liturgy the priest blesses the congregation with the remains of the Body and Blood in the chalice, which is covered in a red corporal. On Good Friday, when Mass may not be celebrated, the Eastern Church still celebrates the "Mass of the Presanctified"—the Mass of the gifts "consecrated the day before". The sacrificial character of the liturgy is actually much more emphatic than in the Latin, even if one compares it with the Latin liturgy prior to Vatican II. When the Hosts are prepared (which in Orthodoxy takes place at the very beginning of the rite, behind the iconostasis, without any participation of the people), the pieces of bread selected for transubstantiation are pierced with a tiny lance, just as Jesus' side was pierced by a lance on Golgotha. The procession with the as yet unconsecrated Offertory gifts attracts the greatest possible reverence. The priest carries wine and bread, magnificently veiled, through the church, preceded by a thurifer walking backward and constantly incensing the gifts. Depending on the particular congregation, people either bow profoundly or kneel, foreheads touching the ground, as the unconsecrated gifts pass by. Here the Host is treated like an as yet uncrowned monarch, proceeding to his coronation, accompanied by all the appropriate gestures of reverence. The Copts, after the Consecration, even use a fan, wafting a breeze toward the consecrated Host, no doubt also to banish the flies, as one would in the presence of a physical monarch. Such ceremonial fans were still in use in the West in medieval times, but the Copts' practice goes back to the earliest days of Christianity.

The Christian religion owes two of its most important institutions to Egyptian Christians: the definition of Mary as Mother of God and monasticism. From the Copts, even today, one can find out how the early Christians behaved toward the Host: nothing can be more authentic than this. Anyone going to Communion fasts for a day beforehand and keeps continent in marriage. He takes off his shoes, for the sanctuary is "holy ground" and the Host was prefigured in the burning bush: it is the Bread of Life, remaining undiminished however many are fed by it. Communion is received in the mouth, and then a cloth (Augustine calls it the *dominicale*) is pressed to the mouth, and the communicant goes to the next priest, who administers the Precious Blood. This cloth is later rinsed according to the same rules described above in connection with the corporal and purificator.

Both Coptic and Greek Orthodox rites contain a custom that is highly instructive as regards the special nature of the Host. During the Consecration large bowls full of pieces of bread are brought and held over the transubstantiated sacrificial gifts. This bread, the so-called *antidoron*, is distributed to everyone after the liturgy: people go up to the priest, kiss his hand and the bread, and either eat it in the church or bring it home to those who could not be present. This bread is not the Host: it is blessed bread, holy bread, but not the Lord's Body; people can receive it without prior preparation, and, though it carries a blessing from the altar, it is "common food" all the same. In these oriental churches there can never be any confusion as to where Holy Communion ends and the community's love feast begins.

I can imagine that all these details of rites, probably alien to you, may produce a feeling of bewilderment and even irritation. You may have been expecting a reflection on the theology of the Last Supper or a discussion of the Catholic and the Protestant ways of looking at the mysteries of Holy Thursday. Well, I am not a theologian. As a storyteller, I am infinitely more fascinated by what I see than by ideas, however profound. Ideas can swell up and fill the entire interior cosmos—and then evaporate like a mist. Just when you thought you had grasped some idea or other, it vanishes into thin air. For me, observed reality has an entirely different weight, particularly when I do not understand it.

As a writer, I would never dream of writing a novel about human rights or human dignity or their philosophical and religious foundations. I would always try to depict people, people who retain their dignity and people who lose it. People whose nature shows them to be securely embedded in the cosmos, and others who drift around in it, lost, utterly unable to claim any rights for themselves. When I discovered that the Host was venerated like a king (one must never turn one's back on a king but must walk backward when leaving his presence) and, moreover, that it was treated with a respect that quite clearly included fear, this reverence made a profound impression on me. I cannot understand how people who have been brought up with this kind of reverence could ever dream of abandoning it—unless they have undergone a severe crisis of faith.

When I think of the abolition of the worship and veneration of the Host after Vatican II—just as in the centuries following the Reformation—a military image always presents itself to me, perhaps because military ceremonial still retains its sign language, to some extent. What I see is the degradation of Captain Dreyfus, so vividly described by a number of writers. After being convicted as a German spy, he had to appear in full uniform in front of his regiment to hear his sentence. His punishment not only meant prison on the island of Cayenne: he also forfeited his military rank. The officer who pronounced the sentence next demanded that Dreyfus surrender his sword. The Captain's sword was broken over the officer's thigh; the shards were thrown at the feet of the supposed traitor. Then Dreyfus' epaulettes were torn from his shoulders and his emblems of rank from his breast.

To me, it is exactly the same when I see people still on their feet in front of the elevated Host, when I see them entering a church without genuflecting, and receiving Communion in their outstretched hands. I, myself, see it as a degradation, a pointed, symbolic refusal to give honor. Incidentally, Communion in the hand is inappropriate, not because the hands are less worthy to receive the Host than the tongue, for instance, or because they might be dirty, but because it would be impossible to rinse every participant's hands after Communion (that is, to make sure no particles of the Host are lost).

It was through the signs of reverence I saw from early childhood that the Host became, for me, what the Church's tradition claims it to be: a Living Being. From that time on, the presence of this Living Being triumphed over every doubt (and of course my faith in Christ has not been free from doubt). I find it hard to speak about my faith or my unbelief. For Christians it is axiomatic that one's faith must be professed, but I feel that there is just as much to be said for hiding it. Whenever I said publicly that I believed in God, I always felt guilty afterward. All of a sudden it seemed a lie, or at least so oversimplified as to become untrue. The biblical paradox "Lord, I believe, help thou my unbelief" sums up everything that is to be said on the topic of faith. Furthermore, "unbelief" is in many cases (and this is true in my case) far too strong a word. For the most part, what we are talking about is God becoming, in a way, invisible; the truths of faith fade, become less substantial, less real. There is nothing heroic about this kind of unbelief: it is a kind of spiritual paralysis, a temporary loss of metaphysical vigor. I incline toward the view of the great Rumanian nihilist Emile Cioran, who was convinced that genuine unbelief is just as rare as genuine faith: most people are swimming in the vast gray sea in between, from time to time getting nearer the one coast or the other.

The Presence of God Is Terrifying

So I am not laying claim to be any kind of spiritual athlete when I say that, even at times when God and the Church seemed to have disappeared over the horizon as far as I was concerned, I never stopped believing in the sacredness of the Host. I continued to believe in the sacredness of the Host even at times when I fundamentally doubted the possibility of there being anything sacred at all. Even in those days when religion had entirely vanished from my mind, I would never have touched a consecrated Host or a chalice, or listened to observations on art history in front of the tabernacle.

It is very clear to me that this practical belief in the Host even in times of unbelief is probably a fruit of my early experience and practice of veneration of the Host. Faith may have gone away, but fear remained. Fear has a bad reputation in our times. "Be not afraid!" we are urged from every pulpit and in every religious broadcast. People often forget that the angels need to say "Be not afraid!" because they themselves inspire fear. God's presence is *terribilis*, "fear-inspiring": it is the moment of truth that will make us all tremble. The fear I have of dishonoring the Host, a fear that is deeply rooted at a level below faith, would perhaps, in a solidly religious milieu, be called superstition; but I have learned to apply to it the words of the Old Covenant: "Timor Domini initium sapientiae." For me, this fear is indeed the beginning of wisdom; at all events it is the foundation of my faith.

I have talked about the ritual practice of the faith and the effect on me of such practice. This seemed a truer and more real way of proceeding than to engage in lay theological debate about articles of faith. All the same, I do not wish to avoid the question of faith's actual content. While it is true that, for me, the veneration of the Host is something fundamental, beyond argument, something necessary to my soul and that I do not need to justify; it is also true that it *does* find its justification in that Holy Thursday evening two thousand years ago, when Jesus assembled his disciples in a room furnished with carpets for the purpose. What took place during this assembly has become the subject of an endless debate. Archaeologists, philologists, and philosophers have pored over this event. Attempts to interpret it deeply split Christendom in the wake of the Reformation. Here I do not intend to repeat the ideas put forward by theologians of every hue concerning the nature of the

Last Supper—not even the explanations that are binding on me as a Catholic. I would simply like to set forth my own private—perhaps naïve—way of understanding the Last Supper, at which Jesus ate the Passover lamb with his disciples, as I find it in the Gospels. This interpretation makes no claim to be authoritative.

As well as reading the Gospels as a believing Christian, however, I also read them with the eyes of someone who has read a great many stories. I know how to tell a story; I know what the storyteller's techniques are, and I know how to evaluate a story according to the means it uses, how to allow myself to be drawn into it and into its world. So I see before me the room in which the disciples reclined at table with Jesus; I see them eating their lamb, their ritual meal of sacrifice in memory of the Exodus from Egypt; I see Jesus taking bread in his hands, breaking it, and sharing it with them with these words: "This is my body, which is given for you and for many."

If I ask, not as a believer but as a reader of a literary story, what Jesus could have meant by these words, there is only one answer, an answer that arises from the very spirit of the story itself: he meant them literally. In this story, the man who hands his friends a piece of bread and says it is his body means that he regards this bread as his body, really and truly. He may be insane; but we must not attempt to water down what he says. Perhaps he is a megalomaniac artist like Magritte, who wrote under the picture of a pipe, "ceci n'est pas une pipe" [this is not a pipe]—but he himself believes and means what he says. This was no time, at such a secret, portentous meal with its profoundly serious tone, for subtle symbolism, intellectual puzzles, or pseudo-philosophical language games. I find it impossible to come to any other conclusion, from the context of the Gospels, than that the man reported there meant what he said.

The poet Charles Péguy expressed it similarly in his great poem "The Portal of the Mystery of Hope":

Jesus Christ, my child, did not come to waste the little time
     he had in telling us trifles.
What are three years in the life of a world?
What are three years in the eternity of this world?
He had no time to lose, he did not squander it on tomfoolery
     and guessing games,
intellectual guessing games,
subtle charades,
riddles,
ambiguities and wretched, strained witticisms.
No, he had neither time nor effort to lose.
He didn't have the time.
—Oh, the tremendous efforts he had to make!—
No, he did not prodigally pour out his whole being,
he did not make this vast, terrible self-emptying,
this emptying of himself, of his being, of everything,
and at such a price,
merely to give us coded messages to work out,
tricks to solve, silly pranks, sleight of hand,
clever deceptions like a village sorcerer,
like a country trickster,
like a vagrant fool, like a quack in his cart,
like the local card-sharper, like the most cunning fellow in
     the tavern.[1]

[1] Translated by Graham Harrison from "Le porche de la deuxième vertu", by Charles Péguy, in Œvres poétiques complètes, Collection Bibliothèque de la Pléiade (Paris: Éditions Gallimard, 1957).

Péguy expresses what emerges from the Gospel's literary context, but he also expresses something that goes beyond this context. He calls this man, the man who in all earnest refers to a piece of bread as his body, the Savior, *Salvator mundi*. He professes the Church's faith that Jesus is God's Son, the second Person of the Trinity, who became a creature to rescue the creation. In fact, Holy Week mirrors the six days of creation with astonishing exactness: on the first day of creation, when light was created, Jesus enters Jerusalem in triumph. On Holy Thursday, on the very day the mammals were created, he eats the Easter lamb. On the day when man was created, the God-man (crucified over what, according to an ancient tradition, was the site of Adam's grave) redeemed mankind, which had sinned in Adam. On the day when the Creator God rested, Jesus lay in the tomb. Then, on Easter morning, there begins the new creation of a humanity that is now able to free itself from its inherited burden of guilt.

God Himself Said That This Bread Is His Body

Jesus of Nazareth, according to the Chalcedonian Creed, is "born of the Father before all time, God from God, Light from Light, true God from true God, of one substance with the Father", and it concludes by saying that all things are created by him. In the Church's faith, the God who created the world is identical with the man who, two thousand years ago in Jerusalem, asserted that a piece of bread was his body. It is God's thoughts and God's words that create reality. Reality is what God calls by its name: light, darkness, water and air, man and beast. The new creation, however, is no longer a creation out of nothing. It is a healing of the old creation and consists of transformations and metamorphoses. God becomes man; and then he becomes mere matter, serving as nourishment for man and divinizing him.

The Colombian philosopher Nicolas Gomez Davila expressed Jesus Christ's relationship to the Gospel in the following way: "If the Gospels have any meaning, Jesus of Nazareth must be the Son of God. But if Jesus is the Son of God, we need a Christology that far transcends the Gospels." At all events, for those of us gathered here, the Gospel has a meaning that far transcends any world-view or philosophy. None of the committed followers of Socrates, inspired by the life and death of this great man, ever had the idea of assembling on the anniversary of his death and sacrificing a cock, as, shortly before the great man expired, he had requested his pupil Kriton to do. Anyone who goes to church on Holy Thursday believes he knows the identity of the man who broke bread in the Upper Room at the Last Supper. And if God says that this bread is his Body, there is only one response man can offer: he must worship this bread.

Appendix 2

The Missal of Trent

Anyone examining the magnificent masterpieces of Western bookcraft, the evangeliaria and ritualia, Lectionaries and Missals, and the so-called Books of Hours used in the Church's prayer; anyone who admires the illuminated books and precious bindings and is fascinated by the different scripts and the typographical organization of the pages will be tempted to see them as autonomous works of art that, like buildings or statues, fulfill their function in life largely by simply being there. However, viewing even the most astonishing of all these books as they lie open in their glass cases is like looking at a famous female dancer embalmed in a glass coffin: her present condition gives no clue to her former life and mastery of the stage. For these books were not simply places for conserving texts: they were acting persons, as it were, in the wider and narrower public spheres. They exercised a creative influence, and, by radiating far beyond themselves, they generated an entire cosmos in artistic motion. They not only contained the rules of this cosmos and enshrined its corpus of legislation: like major planets, they were also part of it. None of this comes to mind, however, when one sees them as items in a museum, abstracted from their real life and kept in air-conditioned and shock-proof rooms, in tomblike silence—but utterly remote from their sacral context. Moreover, very many connoisseurs and lovers of these noble books have no idea that the very life to which they gave rise, and which then nourished and animated them in return, still exists today: the tradition of these rites and ceremonies continues unbroken and has done so for almost two thousand years. It is strange to realize that it was only in 1968 that the Catholic Church endeavored to cut loose from the tradition of her rites, which until then had developed organically in her womb from the earliest beginnings down to the present. The most severe verdict on the new Mass promulgated by Pope Paul VI, against the urgent advice of many bishops, was given by then Cardinal Ratzinger, now Pope Benedict XVI, when he said—going even farther than the then Patriarch of Constantinople—that "a liturgy that had grown organically had been pushed aside in favor of a fabricated liturgy." [1] Since 1968 the classical rite has been largely suppressed by the bishops of the Catholic Church; those who continue to adhere to it are regarded with suspicion as obscurantist reactionaries. Nonetheless the old rite has not ceased to exist; Pope John Paul II himself allowed the old books to be brought into use again, and the old rite is celebrated in small chapels in many places. This means that those who so desire can again experience the ambience of the wonderful old Missals and breathe their atmosphere. A detailed study would be required to show why, for the Catholic Church, an attack on her rites has almost fatal consequences—but space forbids. In a nutshell one could say that the Catholic religion is the religion of the divine Incarnation: according to her Founder's will, she continues to live this divine Incarnation—in ever new experience—in her sacraments and the rites that

---

[1] Preface to the French edition of K. Gamber, *La Réforme liturgique en question* (Le Barroux: Éditions Sainte-Madeleine, 1992), p. 8.

express them; for this reason these sacraments and rites must be most strictly kept aloof from all subjectivism and all private and personal inspiration. God alone can guarantee his presence in the rite: our protestations to this effect are fruitless, as are our attempts to lay down the conditions under which his presence manifests itself. The entire religious wisdom of the Jewish and Gentile world went into the creation of the Church's rites; the apostles and martyrs laid their foundations. The language of the Church, the Latin language she created to preserve her treasure, was uniquely apt to define the articles of faith. As regards the future of the old rites, the last word has not been spoken. The reign of Pope Benedict prompts one to hope that the old rite will be allowed to prosper. At all events the Pope will try to go farther than his predecessor in promoting them.

It follows, then, that in speaking of the Roman Missal I shall not be referring to the Missal promulgated by Pope Paul VI in 1968, the so-called *Novus ordo*. I can ignore this new Mass in good conscience, since the modern clergy, for the most part, do not keep to the *Novus ordo* anyway, preferring to stand at the altar with a loose-leaf folder of privately composed prayers and quotations from Saint-Exupéry's *Little Prince*. Nor shall I deal with the early medieval codices that were created when Christian culture was approaching that particular zenith. What is now called the Missal was then distributed among several complementary books. The schola sang from the Gradual, named after the *gradus*, the "steps", since it contains the processional chants of the Introit, the Gradual itself, the Offertory, and Communion. The Scripture readings were taken from the Lectionary, containing pericopes from Paul's Epistles and the Gospels. The celebrant at the altar had a book containing the Canon of the Mass. In addition, however, there were books with processional chants and Benedictionals with blessings, forming a constellation around the Mass liturgy itself. It may seem somewhat bizarre if I now set aside these books and their extraordinary artistic perfection and concentrate instead on a book that can indeed lay claim to beauty in the realm of typography, but seems paler, more technical, and rationalistic than its predecessors. In the Middle Ages, indeed, people did begin putting the various books required for Mass into a single volume, but this Missal—that is, a book that contains all the parts of the liturgy—did not attain its comprehensive form until the Council of Trent. This great reforming Council took the Mass of the Roman Pontiff, unchanged from ancient times and proof against all heretical influence, and made it a universally binding liturgy; for this purpose it created a book in which, as in a Noah's Ark, all the cultic regulations were codified and collated. Compared with the gorgeous illumination of the medieval codices, the Missal of Trent attests a dogged sobriety of religious scepticism in the midst of a world that had descended into chaos. The Tridentine Missal no longer assumes that there is an all-pervading Catholic culture that supports the cult because it springs from it. Of course, the spirit of the Catholic rite is purely distilled in the Roman basilica or the French cathedral or the blazing gold of a Spanish altar— but it is found equally in that World War II Mass-chest I recently saw being used: it had battered corners and was the size of a large typewriter case; the lid opened to reveal the Mass cards stuck to its inner side; a folding panel containing a saint's relic (the *sepulcrum*) could be laid over the bottom half of the chest; it contained a chalice as small as an egg cup, Mass cruets in a leather pouch, an *aspergillum* the size of a fountain pen, the Missal in the format of a prayer book, the priest's stole like a violet silk ribbon for wrapping presents, and a small nickel standing crucifix with matching candlesticks: this chest that seems to proclaim "Omnia mea mecum porto", this doll's altar that can be set up anywhere, is equally the epitome, the essential expression of the Roman cult and, most particularly, of the Tridentine Missal. For here the attempt is made to pack the entire fullness of Catholic faith and practice into a nutshell—albeit a fairly fat one sometimes. The Missal of Trent is certainly made for the cathedral, but also for the jungle, for the most remote and forgotten diaspora chapel and for the Catacombs. It is a Robinson Crusoe traveling set: a priest, shipwrecked on a remote island with nothing but the Missal of Trent, could produce, with it, the whole patrimony of Catholicism.

It belongs to the Catholic faith to endeavor to express the truth in irreducible paradoxes; and it is one of these paradoxes that, while Catholicism is not a book religion, it cannot find a better and more meaningful way of expressing this fact than in a book—the Missal. Holy Scripture is present in this Missal—in the selection of pericopes, translated into Latin, and in virtue of the context in which they are set (for instance, the way in which Old and New Testaments reciprocally explain one another); but tradition is also present, it too understood as revelation; and finally there is the revelation of the sacraments—Christ's healing and blessing presence, mediated through the Church. Rightly or wrongly, the Catholic Church fears nothing so much as having her rites associated with magic and magical practices. All the same, we can be quite sure that the idea of the book of spells, such as Shakespeare's Prospero has kept by him in his lonely banishment, the book that makes him a master of spirits, cut off as he is from all earthly resources, is drawn from the concrete example of the Roman Missal. In what follows I shall try to portray the life of the Missal and describe its role in the world for which it was created— and which the Missal has itself shaped.

The Content of the Missal of Trent

Anyone who opens any edition of the Tridentine Missal, be it from the eighteenth, nineteenth, or twentieth century, will immediately be attracted by the beauty of the typography. The texts are presented in two columns per page, printed in Antiqua typeface; all the headings, psalm references, the texts that are not prayers, and the line between the two columns are printed in red: this manifests a typographical taste that carried over into secular book design—one thinks of the novels published in France by Gallimard or the German weekly *Die Zeit*. A Missal is usually big, and its print is also large and easily legible, even when the light of the celebrant's eyes is beginning to fail. A Missal begins with the Bulls of Popes Pius V, Clement VII, Urban VIII, and Pius X, who published the latest editions with modifications particularly regarding the Calendar. Next comes the major part of the Calendar, containing a complicated calendar of feasts and saints, with its concurrences. The degree of knowledge required—how to work out the order of priority of the various celebrations that can occur on the same day, which feast has to give way to another or is merely "commemorated", which feast retains its precedence—is quite terrifying and would call for the passion for order of a Chinese court major-domo. Next comes a long section with the *Ritus servandus*, the instructions concerning the preparation of the altar and the way Mass is to be celebrated. This is followed by the prayers that are to be said before the Mass, particularly those said by the priest as he puts on the vestments. Then there are diagrams showing the sequence and manner of incensations using blessed incense. Next come the proper Mass texts for the feasts between Advent and Easter. Roughly in the middle of the fat Missal there is the most important part, used daily, that is, the fixed parts of the Mass. After this come the Sundays from Easter to the Last Sunday after Pentecost, followed by the many and diverse Masses of the saints for the whole ecclesiastical year from November 29 until November 26 of the following year. The Common of Saints contains generic Masses for saints who have no special Mass formulary, arranged in every conceivable category. Here one finds the Mass for a "Virgin not a martyr" beside that for a "Martyr not a virgin" and that for a saint "neither virgin nor martyr". Next we come to the large number of Votive Masses for every imaginable circumstance on earth, in heaven, and in purgatory: here we find (even after World War II) a Mass for the Roman Emperor, a Mass in time of earthquake, a Mass for rain, and one for the avoidance of bad weather, a Mass for the gift of tears, for the gift of patience, a Mass for enemies, for travelers, and for prisoners. Finally we have the Masses for the Dead, followed by blessings for the altar vessels and for holy water. A Missal is a thick book, with at least 850 pages, and a heavy one: two hands are required to carry it.

Regulations concerning the Missal

The Missal has its special place on the altar, initially on the right side (seen from the congregation), the *cornu epistulae*, or "Epistle side". This is where it stands from the beginning of Mass until after the reading of the Epistle. Then it is moved to the left side, the "Gospel side", where not only the Gospel is read, but also the Offertory prayers and, most important of all, the core of the sacrificial ritual, the Canon of the Mass. Today, mostly, the Missal sits on a small wooden stand that should be covered with a cloth of the liturgical color of the particular feast. This stand is a help, enabling the celebrant to read without difficulty, but it is not a classic item of altar furniture. The Missal's rubrics actually specify a cushion (*cussinus*) for the Book to rest on. Liturgical dictionaries often tend to trace liturgical prescriptions back to some practical requirement or other; thus one reads that the cushion was used to protect the Missal from wear and tear, since it was often a very costly volume encased in ivory carving and inlaid with gold or precious stones. We should almost always be suspicious of these attempts to derive practices from profane utility. Sometimes they may be correct regarding one particular aspect of a prescription, but the latter's real character is always sacral. Often enough the prosaic function and its sacral nature are not mutually exclusive anyway. Ancient sacrificial practice is connected by a thousand filaments to the customs of daily life: it cites them, sublimates them, and elevates them into the transcendent context that claims to be the genuine reality of the world. In the oriental world the cushion signifies the royal throne. The Sultan receives the great personages of his realm on a cushion-filled divan; here he pronounces law; here he is visibly the monarch. The Missal is enthroned on a cushion like just such a monarch; the colored silk cloth that, in the West, covers the Missal stand gives a distant hint of this royal cushion, of this Solomon's divan. Interestingly, whenever the book is shut, the cut foreedge is always toward the middle of the altar, in spite of the fact that the Missal is not itself arranged like a Semitic book; this is possibly a faint memory of oriental customs.

At a pontifical Mass, where the Gospel was not sung by the priest at the altar but by a deacon in the sanctuary, the old basilicas often had a special pulpit for the singing of the Gospel. Here the *evangeliarium*, the Book of the Gospels, was laid on a stand in the form of a bronze eagle, which held the book on its wings. The psalms repeatedly mention God's "wings" that are spread in protection over mankind. These bronze eagles also remind us of the imperial eagle, but also of the eagle of Jupiter and the eagle symbolizing John the Evangelist. The message that is proclaimed to us comes from above, on eagle's wings; we are meant to experience it winging its way to us earthly mortals from the realms of everlasting light.

In abbeys and collegiate churches, but also in cathedrals, that is, in churches where a large choir performed the Propers (the chants belonging to the day's feast), there used to be a high iron or wooden stand for the huge folio volume from which the chant was sung. This custom lasted for a long time but is now very rare. While the priest read the appropriate prayers quietly, the choir had this portion of the Missal before their eyes, written in very large notes and letters that could be read from a distance. The singer's posture was not introverted: each singer did not look at his own individual book—the *Liber usualis* known to us today—but looked up to follow the one book that hovered above the whole schola. Both music and words came to them from above, and they responded to these sounds, thus translated into signs, with their own chanting. The chant arose to heaven and also came down from heaven. The later development of organ Masses and orchestral Masses, with mixed choirs singing from galleries, performing the contemporary art music in the Mass, was bound to bring about a certain weakening of that radical liturgical attitude according to which nothing was to be heard at Mass except what was written and laid down in the Missal. Grouped around the high stand for the Gradual, the singers were clearly visible and audible as liturgical functionaries who, by their singing, shared in the priestly office. No one would have ever had the idea that the chanting of the liturgically robed singers around the great Gradual book was a musical adornment of the ceremonies, a decoration that could be added, omitted, or changed at will. This chant was an integral part of the Sacrifice, incarnating it, so to speak. And although the Gradual was there as a separate book extracted from the Missal, there was no sense of a hiatus between it and the supremely important book on the altar. It was as if the one book could be present in the sanctuary in several and various forms.

When the deacon announces the Gospel at the pontifical High Mass, the subdeacon usually holds the book for him. Holding the book in this way is surely the most expressive way of showing the book's majestic position. Man becomes a book-rest. The subdeacon holds the open book at head height and supports it against his forehead. Forehead and hands become the book's throne. Man bows beneath the book in an attitude that bespeaks renunciation of the will, indebtedness, and submission. Here we see most clearly that, during the Mass, the book is treated as a living being.

There are two other objects associated with the book during the rite. In the pontifical Mass the celebrating bishop has an assistant at his side, the *presbyter assistens*, who does not wear Mass vestments but choir dress, a cope (*pluviale*). This priest's task is to guide the bishop through the Missal, turning the pages and indicating the next prayers to be said. In former times he used a small rod for this purpose, a metal scepter ending in a tiny hand and extended index finger. Interestingly, a very similar pointing-stick is used when reading the Torah in the orthodox Jewish service. It may seem puzzling at first that prelates who spend their whole lives in and with the liturgy cannot find their way around the Missal on their own; but we begin to see that this ritual of pointing actually manifests the celebrant's submission to the traditional order of prayer: it is not something created by him. Here again the cult wishes to be understood and experienced as something given, not made by the man of the moment. The celebrant is an instrument, just as the pointing-stick is. When the Mass is celebrated by an ordinary priest, the "master of ceremonies" indicates the relevant places in the Missal with his entire hand, not, of course, with the index finger; this pointing is very closely associated with the use of the Missal: of the thousand possibilities contained in it, the pointer "from above" indicates the particular reality applicable to the day. As for the subordinate gestures of the hand on the part of lower clerics and even laymen, they always have a reference to the ministry of the angels. Indicating the correct place in the Missal partakes—most definitely—of the character of revelation.

The second object from the bishop's Mass is equally revelatory and, literally, illuminating in the context of the Missal: this is the candlestick that is held by a special altar server (called *bugiarius*) while the bishop is reading from the Missal. This additional candle may have had a very ordinary purpose at one time, but since the great pontifical Masses (apart from Christmas midnight and the Easter ceremonies) always take place in the bright light before midday, the spiritual meaning of this extra candle, the *bugia*, must have predominated at a very early stage: this candle signifies that the sacred texts are not self-explanatory; the reader's intellect must be set alight, as it were, if they are to be rightly understood. Both the liturgical "pointing" and the candle express a rule that emerges quite naturally from the situation I have described: the celebrant must read out all the prayers from the page even if he feels he knows them by heart.

The bishop is indeed an "illuminated" person, but this illumination is not due to diligent study and ascetical perfection on his part. It is added to him from outside, as a gift: it is not something merited. The *bugia* also means that the collection of prayers in the Missal cannot be understood as automatic formulae, carrying out the user's intentions like magic spells. The little candlesticks on the bishop's cathedra show that the best things in the Missal remain hidden and that the Missal remains a closed book unless it is read in the correct light, a light that cannot be manipulated.

The Veneration of the Missal

The veneration accorded to the Missal during the liturgy is expressed right from the outset in its costly exterior. One finds bindings that are like miniature architectural structures; constructed of expensive materials and decorated with carved figures, they resemble holy relics reposing in ostensories. The Missal becomes a tiny cathedral into which, opening it, one enters. In the liturgy a characteristic way of showing reverence is the procession. Here customs of the ancient world, religious and profane, live on even in the present time. After all, we are still acquainted with the triumphal parade of victorious troops or the entry of a state visitor into a city decorated in his honor. The procession is a sign of eminence, an affirmation of royal dignity. Together with the priest, preceded in the pontifical Mass by the deacon holding the book aloft, the Missal makes its own *joyeuse entrée* into the church. Signs of the presence of Christ the King are the candles and incense: at the solemn entrance they relate, above all, to the priest who embodies Christ;

but they also relate to the book, which brings Christ's presence about. In the pontifical Mass there is yet another procession—the Gospel procession. As the Gradual and Alleluia are sung, the deacon goes to the celebrant to be commissioned by him to read the Gospel. He kneels to receive the celebrant's blessing and kisses his hand; then a long procession forms up right to the edge of the sanctuary, consisting of acolytes, thurifers, subdeacon, and deacon. It is organized in such a way that the deacon, between two candles, sings the Gospel toward the north, not toward the west (that is, where the congregation is): the north is the abode of pagans, and the Good News is broadcast to them through the walls of the church. For the assembled congregation, however, the Gospel is principally a manifestation of the teaching Christ, a sacramental absolution of sins—"per evangelica dicta deleantur nostra delicta"—and a blessing. A cross is painted or printed at the start of the Gospel passage set for the particular day: it indicates the place to be kissed by the deacon after he has read or sung the Gospel; after this the subdeacon carries the book to the bishop, sitting on his throne (or to the celebrant waiting at the altar) and holds it out for him to kiss.

Incensing the book is also an ancient sign of veneration. Incense has many meanings in the Mass: it is a sign of the presence of the invisible God, as in the Holy of Holies in the Jerusalem Temple; it is an incense offering such as used to be made in the Temple, preceding the burnt offering that was fulfilled in the sacrifice of Christ; it is a cleansing of sinners (in the incensation of the congregation), a royal mark of respect for the celebrant, and a sign of homage to the Missal.

Strictly speaking, there is no veneration involved in the rite's prescription that, at the beginning of Mass, the priest should open the book at the altar and arrange the *signacula*, the ribbons that mark the relevant places for the feast of the day. It does show, however, that there are meant to be no profane moments when the Missal is in use, no "backstage" preparations. Opening and closing the book are priestly actions. A different kind of time begins when the book is opened. Words, action, and movement well up from it; between the back and front covers of this book the Temple of the New Covenant is fully built up, accessible to everyone, provided a priest is there to do what the book says.

Rubrics

The most precious pages of the old *evangeliaria*, that is, the beginning of Saint John's Gospel, were colored purple, with lettering in gold. Purple, the imperial color, was utterly appropriate for these sublime words. We discern a hint of the Incarnation of the Immaterial One even in the material of the book: the thick color creates a convex surface on the page, creating a kind of relief. In the Missal of Trent the purple has become the red ink that is used for all the parts of the text that are not prayers but instructions about the physical posture to be adopted when saying them. We could call these passages in red the "stage directions". They are called rubrics because they are printed in red. Many people regard the rubrics as the most distinctive—and most problematical—feature of the old Missal. People felt they needed to emancipate themselves from rubrics. Among those who advocate liturgical reform, the word "rubricism" is a pejorative term. Rubricism stands for a liturgy where all subjectivism, all charismatic enthusiasm, all creative inventiveness has been condemned to silence. Rubricism subordinates the celebrant to a strict regime, even in the smallest details of bodily posture. "Oculis demissis,

incessu gravi, corpore erecto"—this is how the priest is to
approach the altar: "with eyes lowered, with dignified step,
body held erect". It is impossible to give an idea of the whole
range of the regulations here; I take at random just one passage from chapter 3 of the *Ritus servandus*, entitled "De Prin-
cipio missae et Confessione facienda":

> When the priest crosses himself he always lays his left hand
> on his breast; when giving other blessings at the altar, bless-
> ing the Offertory gifts or anything else, he lays his left hand
> on the altar, unless something else is prescribed. When cross-
> ing himself he turns the inner side of his right hand toward
> himself, with all the fingers aligned, and stretches out his
> hand. He makes a cross from forehead to breast and from
> left shoulder to right. However, when he blesses other per-
> sons or things, he indicates with his little finger the person
> or thing he is blessing.

Thus arises the tradition of blessing we find depicted in
many works of art: the index and middle finger are raised,
and the little finger points down; this is not the artist's invention but an ancient rule. There are many rules, too, even
for the way the priest robes himself for Mass: he is even
instructed which sleeve of the alb he should enter first. He
must take the stole with both hands and kiss it before putting it around the back of his neck. The amice, according
to what is laid down in the Book of Leviticus, the Old
Testament's book of rubrics, is first put over the head before
allowing it to fall to the shoulders.

It is in the nature of the rubrics to envisage all imaginable mishaps that could impede the course of the Mass: the
death of the priest before, during, or after transubstantiation; poisoning of the altar wine; fire; the arrival of enemy
troops; flood; severe frost that causes the wine to freeze in

the chalice; and the priest's vomiting after receiving Communion. There is positively nothing that could shake the spirit of the rubrics! They take into account every kind of disturbance of mind or body and have detailed, carefully weighed answers for all eventualities. Comparing this with the mentality of recent centuries, one can understand that rubrics came to be felt as a restricting corset, an artificial barrier. Public prayer, not the prayer of the individual but of the Church's whole Mystical Body, possessed a binding quality that, in an atmosphere of emancipation from all pressure whatsoever, could be felt as a kind of dictatorship. Now, however, after more than a century of the destruction of forms in art, literature, architecture, politics, and religion, too, people are generally beginning to realize that loss of form—almost always—implies loss of content. Rubrics that, at some particular time in history, may have presented an obstacle to this or that individual in his spiritual life could actually promote this spirituality today. One finds that the harshest critics of Catholic practice accept unquestioningly the very strict rules of prayer taught by Asian religions. It has also been forgotten that the great mystics of the past never felt rubrics to be a burden. Even the twentieth century had a great mystical saint, Padre Pio, from Apulia, who was given the stigmata and, with his five bleeding wounds, read the Mass in iron submission to the rubrics. Formerly, seminarians learned rubrics so well they could perform them in their sleep. Just as pianists have to practice hard to acquire some technique that is initially a pure torture, but ultimately sounds like free improvisation, experienced celebrants used to move to and fro at the altar with consummate poise; the whole action poured forth as if from a single mold. These celebrants were not hemmed in by armor-plated rubrics, as it were: they floated on them as if on clouds.

It would be easy to translate the individual rubrical prescriptions, for example, the extending and joining of the priest's hands, into silent prayers. The fact that the Latin Church did not do this *expressis verbis* follows from her juridical sobriety, which valued the integrity of the form more highly than the individual's participation in it (however devout or intense such participation may have been). The Roman approach to form does not assume that the participant at the liturgy is a spiritual genius: it knows it has to do with weak, distracted human beings who are not, generally speaking, filled with a longing for the vision of God and yet are meant to enjoy the unabridged benefits of the blessings brought by God's presence. The rubrics aim to make visible those things that are always there but cannot be seen by us, with our closed senses and hardened hearts. This aim rests on the conviction that even the lifeless world of objects and the spiritless world of bodies can nonetheless share in God's reality and be a vehicle for his radiance, once they are set within the correct context. "You, creature of water" and "you, creature of salt"—this is how the priest addresses these soulless substances when preparing holy water at the beginning of Sunday Mass; this water and salt are thus destined to return to the primal holiness of all objects and elements at the beginning of the world, when all water was holy because God's Spirit was resting on it.

The Book with Seven Seals

The Apocalypse, Saint John's "hidden revelation", this vast poetic display of uniquely impressive images that have entered into the imagination of entire peoples, has produced an endless ocean of interpretations, nourished hermetic teachings, and spawned political utopias. The Apocalypse's wealth of

images has been differently interpreted in each epoch of
the history of ideas: clearly, the key used by philology and
the study of the ancient world in its attempt to unlock this
inexhaustible book was very different from the key used by
medieval man, his mind so fertile in pictures. Here we cannot go into the value, theological justification, and schol-
arly weight of the various modes of interpretation. There
are people, however, with a childlike and receptive approach,
who will always be right in their interpretation because they
complement the riddling image with an image of their own
that comes from a fundamental conviction, namely, that even
the most spiritual vision can always be set in relation to the
concrete earthly reality. Thus the early Church understood
the Apocalypse as the liturgical book of the New Testament and, in forming her liturgy, drew her inspiration from
the stupendous portrayals of the "Marriage of the Lamb"—
the super-temporal, eternal liturgy of heaven. Convinced
that microcosm and macrocosm must ultimately agree, the
Church recognized the four winged living creatures as the
spirits of the four Evangelists, and the Book with Seven
Seals as their joint work. However, anyone who has seen
the mosaics, the frescoes, and the illuminations of book artists representing the Book with Seven Seals lying on a
cushion is bound to think of the Missal, its seven broad
marker-ribbons hanging from it just like the seals that hang
from the book in Saint John's vision. In the Vulgate the
seals are actually termed *signacula*, which is what the Missal's rubrics call its marker-ribbons. The rite in which the
Lamb receives the Book with Seven Seals from the hand of
God, so that he may open them, resembles the ceremony
in which the celebrant commissions the deacon to read the
Gospel, and even the solemn incensing of the book that
follows comes from the Apocalypse. And when we read of

the "silence in heaven when the Lamb opened the seventh seal", are we not bound to think of the Consecration at Mass and the canonical silence that surrounds it? As for the menacing figures and catastrophes that emerge from its pages—the horsemen of the Apocalypse, the sun as dark as sackcloth, and the moon like blood—they only *seem* to break the analogy. For from the opened Missal come, not catastrophes, but a wealth of events, miracles, and movements, of transformation and supernatural presence: that is, the Missal is not only prefigured by the Book with Seven Seals: it actually transcends it. It does not belong to history any more: although it has to fulfill its role amid the vicissitudes of history, it is already beyond this history. When we acknowledge the Book with Seven Seals to be the Missal, the Church's revealed cult, developed in her inspired tradition, we are making the most important statement about this cult: it is the means whereby men can unite themselves, along with the redeemed creation, to the eternal worship of God—a worship that is always going on in heaven—and participate in it. There is, however, an entirely natural precondition if we are to participate in this heavenly cult: the cult must be felt to be something not humanly fabricated. We must even feel it to be something alien, something that originates in a different sphere. In the old formula of priestly ordination, sidelined after Vatican II, the Mass was described as a *res periculosa*, a "dangerous and fraught undertaking". Far more than Faust's journey "to the Mothers", it is a leaving of time and history whereby we enter into a feast, a feast that has emerged through apocalyptic catastrophe—a mirror of the demonic evil on earth—a feast of wild and terrifying beauty, the beauty of the seven-horned, seven-eyed Lamb in whose blood mankind's clothes are washed white.

BIBLIOGRAPHICAL NOTE

The essay "Eternal Stone Age" (Ewige Steinzeit) was published in the periodical *Kursbuch* (edited 1965–1975 by Hans Magnus Enzensberger). The other pieces in this volume were first published in *Una Voce Korrespondenz*, in Sinn und Form, in the *Frankfurter Allgemeine Zeitung*, and in the bulletin *Pro missa tridentina* of the Laienvereinigung für den klassischen römischen Ritus [Lay association for the classical Roman Rite]. The present volume contains a passage from the final chapter of my novel *Eine lange Nacht*, published by Aufbau Verlag, Berlin, to whom I express particular thanks for permission to reprint it here.

This third edition has been expanded to include the essay "Revelation through Veiling in the Old Roman Catholic Liturgy".

I thank Robert Gernhardt for permission to print his poem "Saint Horten", Bernhard Carolus for tracing material on Saint Raphael's church, Heidelberg, and Berhard Uske for his editorial work on the texts and much important advice.

[The essay "This Is My Body", presented in appendix 1, was given first as a talk on the veneration of the sacred Host in the Protestant city church of Darmstadt on Holy Thursday 2004; it was later printed for the Feast of Corpus Christi in *Die Tagespost*, June 8, 2004. It as well as the essay on the Missal of Trent in appendix 2 are being added to the English translation of the third edition.]